RAIN
DANCING

WHY RATIONAL BEATS RITUAL

19 . 3 . 2015

For Toby

All the best

Henry

RAIN
DANCING

WHY RATIONAL BEATS RITUAL

*HOW RATIONAL MARKETING
CAN MAKE THE DIFFERENCE
THAT'S WORTH MILLIONS*

Glenn Granger

Matador
9 Priory Business Park,
Wistow Road, Kibworth Beauchamp,
Leicestershire. LE8 0RX
Tel: (+44) 116 279 2299
Fax: (+44) 116 279 2277
Email: books@troubador.co.uk
Web: www.troubador.co.uk/matador

ISBN 978 1780884 851

British Library Cataloguing in Publication Data.
A catalogue record for this book is available from the British Library.

Typeset in 11pt Adobe Garamond Pro by Troubador Publishing Ltd, Leicester, UK

Index by Indexing Specialists (UK) Ltd

Matador is an imprint of Troubador Publishing Ltd
Printed and bound in Great Britain by TJ International Ltd, Padstow, Cornwall

Contents

Foreword

What on earth has an Oxford University-trained mathematician got to teach the world of experienced, battle-hardened consumer and business-to-business marketers?

Well, even a quick read of Glenn Granger's brilliant book will answer that question fairly comprehensively.

Glenn and I both went to Oxford, though my studies were in English, while his formed the basis for a numeracy he has since put to very good use. We've both notched up many years of practical marketing experience at the highest level with many different blue chip companies, and we are both passionate believers in the power and the profits to be gained from making marketing more accountable.

But what he has brought to the discussion is an enviable level of statistical, analytical and financial awareness that has far too often been missing from the debate about marketing accountability.

Decisions about marketing budgets and the allocation of scarce resources need to be taken within a framework of facts and data, and that has seldom been available, even in the largest companies.

We have long known that marketing does not enjoy the respect of most other business disciplines. About six years ago, this was confirmed in a startling report, published by Deloitte, that revealed the deep unease that many CEOs and CFOs were feeling about the way their marketing colleagues spent vast sums of money, with what appeared to be an almost total lack of accountability.

But if this survey was a timely warning, it was quickly overtaken by events as the recession forced the issue of marketing accountability ever more insistently towards centre stage.

The result was disastrous, and may even have served to prolong the recession in the UK. As near-panic set in, we saw cost-cutting on a draconian scale. Budgets were slashed, and the marketing community just did not have the tools to explain rationally and quantitatively why such behaviour would inevitably be bad for both revenue and profits.

More recently, a 2010 report by Deloitte and the Chartered Institute of Marketing, entitled *Improving Marketing Effectiveness,* has highlighted the continuing need for radical change.

'Marketing is often the first budget to be cut in times of need,' the report says, quoting the outsider's familiar insult that 'marketing is just jargonised common sense'.

'Marketers need an evidence-based reply to the question "How do we account for or justify marketing investment?".'

The CIM/Deloitte report goes on to deplore marketing's perennial failure to make its case to senior management.

'Customer behaviour ultimately results in sales and impacts the bottom line. Marketers must have the ability to help measure that process and translate it into clear metrics in a business-oriented language that finance and operations understand and respect.'

In my opinion, the book you hold in your hand is a key part of the answer to this problem.

Raindancing is a deceptively short, succinct document,

written in an easy-to-assimilate and engaging style. But it could be a manifesto for revolution.

Glenn Granger's objective has been to take the very best of marketing measurement practice in some of the world's most successful companies and turn it into models, processes and tools that will transform marketing across vast swathes of the business community.

Marketing urgently needs to grasp the nettle of data and analytics if it is going to make the right decisions and get the recognition it deserves. Granger shows us how this is now easily within our grasp. The tools are available and the opportunity is there. All we need to do is take it.

Professor Malcolm McDonald MA (Oxon) MSc PhD D.Litt
Emeritus Professor, Cranfield University School of Management
Visiting Professor at Henley, Warwick, Aston and Bradford Business Schools
Chairman, Brand Finance plc

'Faced with the choice between changing one's mind and proving that there is no need to do so, almost everyone gets busy on the proof'
– J K Galbraith

CHAPTER 1

Let's Get Real

Not one company in fifty knows whether it should increase, cut or reallocate its marketing budgets. Tradition, guesstimates and 'raindancing' are no basis for business decisions. Rational marketing shouldn't be a gimmick. It should be the norm.

Raindancing. What finer career could there be for a young person to embark on?

The training is hard and long and there is a wealth of culture and tradition to be absorbed. But there will always be the satisfaction of knowing that what you do is socially useful. The dances help to keep the wheels of industry turning, to put food on the table, even to keep our countryside the way it is today.

The skills and nuances of raindancing – no-one has ever been clear whether it should be seen as an art or a science – inevitably take years to master. There is a lot more to it than simply using feathers and turquoise to symbolise wind and water. But once the young person is qualified and has a certain amount of basic practical experience under his or her belt, the sky's the limit. As a valued and respected member of society, the dancer can expect to reap the rewards for early application and effort for decades to come.

It is important to note, too, that raindancing involves no expensive technology, unlike the silver iodide cloud-seeding techniques the Chinese used, for example, to control Beijing's weather during the 2008 Olympics (or the Russian air force's recently-used method, which involves dumping sacks of cement into the clouds). Raindancing is there for everyone, regardless of means.

There are moral issues, of course. It is a matter of fine judgment whether it is fair to bless upstream farmers with drought-breaking cloudbursts if this may cause flooding and disruption downstream. But, generally speaking, it is clear that raindancing is mostly harmless.

The only problem with all this is that raindancing simply doesn't work.

There is no causal connection between what goes on at ground level and the rain that may or may not fall in the next few hours or days.

The rituals and ceremonies, the carefully observed traditions, the training and effort, the discussion and chanting, the earnest prayers and fervent hopes – they are all in vain.

And, unfortunately, to a much greater extent than anyone is prepared to admit, the same often applies to marketing.

Our marketing activity undoubtedly has a substantial impact on the external world. But the truth is that we usually don't know in advance what these impacts will be. Worse still, we frequently can't tell what they have been, even after the event.

There is not one company in ten that has any scientific way of distinguishing the effects of its advertising campaigns from the simultaneous impacts of heatwaves, competitor advertising or price changes.

There is not one company in 50 that can quantify these effects and know, with any certainty at all, whether it should increase, decrease or reallocate its marketing spending to maximise profits.

How do I know these uncomfortable truths?

I have used analytics and advanced modelling around the world for more than 20 years, during which time I have built up a successful sales and marketing modelling consultancy and sold it to one of the great global consultancies, Accenture. I am now involved in developing revolutionary marketing modelling software for the desktop with my present company, marketingQED (www.marketingQED.com).

I have worked with brilliant and inspired marketing brains at most of the leading agencies and run modelling projects for many of the biggest global brands. I have also been one of the technical judges for the prestigious Institute of Practitioners in Advertising (IPA) Effectiveness Awards.

I have seen the reality for myself.

And it's not great.

A lot of this book is concerned with the detailed weaknesses of the way we do and measure marketing today, and with the observations that have made me such an impassioned missionary for the cause of modelling and 'rational marketing'.

But the most important parts are those that try to spell out the immense potential that is available to us in this area.

Without necessarily changing anything else about the way we do business, we can use modelling to make marketing more cost-effective, to avoid waste, to save millions and to make millions.

This is not a textbook on how to use statistics to improve business performance. I have deliberately included a bare minimum of explanation about the theory behind analytics and modelling and a good deal of practical advice on how the new tools that are just becoming available can be used.

I believe the introduction of powerful, easy-to-use desktop modelling software will quickly transform the way marketing departments operate. For big companies, it will make it possible to use real-time modelling as an everyday decision support tool. For smaller companies, it will make analytics, modelling, forecasting and budget optimisation tools available for the first time.

No-one would vote for irrational marketing. The very idea is preposterous. But rational marketing is not what we see around us today.

It is time to end the raindancing. It is time to stop guessing and use the data we have about past performance to make rational, fact-based predictions about the future, and better decisions now, in the present.

We need to establish real connections between what we do and the results we get. We've got to stop mistaking coincidence for causality.

We need to drop the long-held myths about what works and what doesn't and re-examine our habits and conventions in the light of the data that's readily available to us. We need to understand about response curves and profit curves and learn what they tell us about squeezing the last drop of profit out of the marketing pound or dollar.

We need to stop doing the raindance and hoping for the best. We need to start making things happen the way we want them to, through the use of rational optimisation techniques and day-to-day support for our decision-making processes.

We need to get real. And we need to start now.

*'I thus claim to show, not how men think in myths,
but how myths operate in men's minds without
their being aware of the fact'
— Claude Lévi-Strauss*

CHAPTER 2

Why Marketing Gets it Wrong

Trusting in intuition, luck and the occasional miraculous coincidence is not good enough. Small groups make big mistakes and perpetuate myths that confuse correlation and coincidence with causality. But it doesn't have to be like this.

I believe in rationality. That's what this book is about.

Rationality is not cold, hard and unsentimental. Rationality is a tool we use to understand the way the world works, and the knowledge it gives us helps us move mountains. I'm still lost in wonder when I see nearly 400 tons of jumbo jet leap from a runway and soar up into the sky, to land 13 hours later in Hong Kong or 10 hours later in Vancouver.

The mechanics, the aeronautics, the electronics, the 6 million parts – it is an amazing everyday achievement to bring all this together, fill it with fuel, cargo and people and hurl it across half the world.

This leap into the skies would have seemed like a miracle in earlier times. To us, it's not. We know that it is 'simply' the product of rationality.

I don't believe in fairies, supernatural forces, the Loch Ness monster, divine intervention, raindancing or the lottery favouring the deserving. I believe in the sort of miracles that come about through the miraculous messaging medium of markets, which manage to aggregate the signals and bring together the particles of human genius to create things so complex that no mind can truly take them in.

My other favourite everyday miracle is the supermarket. I'm not fussy. Almost any supermarket will do. I am simply stunned by the logistical and organisational effort that converges on the shelves of every supermarket in the land, bringing us fresh fruit and vegetables from across the globe with such monotonous efficiency that many of our children have no idea that apples and peas, nectarines and ugli fruit are seasonal crops.

There was a true story about Mikhail Gorbachev visiting Canada in 1983, marvelling at the array of produce available in a supermarket and jumping to the conclusion that this extraordinary cornucopia of plenty had been laid on especially to impress him. When he was eventually convinced that, no, this was just normal, he went back to the Soviet Union a chastened man, knowing the writing was on the wall for Communism because it, literally, couldn't deliver.

The daily miracle of the supermarket is a triumph of market forces. This is capitalism at its best, entirely dependent on the millions of tiny transactions, the votes, if you like, of millions of consumers every day. Every transaction sends a message. Someone liked this brand, rather than that. Someone chose the cheaper own label product. Someone shopped in the 24-hour Tesco at 1am.

Those messages come to us as data. Individually, they don't necessarily tell us all that much. Collectively, they tell us everything. But only if we know how to listen.

* * * * *

In 2011, Erik Brynjolfsson and Heekyung Hellen Kim, of the Massachusetts Institute of Technology, and Lorin M Hutt, of the Wharton School at the University of Pennsylvania, presented a conference paper entitled *Strength in Numbers: How Does Data-Driven Decision-Making Affect Firm Performance?*

It has still not been published as this book goes to print, but this is important research.

The idea was not new. As Brynjolfsson pointed out, people had been looking for evidence of the payoffs from using 'data and analysis rather than experience and intuition' for some time. But nobody had got round to pinning down the numbers to back up the anecdotes linking data-driven decision-making (now known in trendy business circles as DDD) to better company performance.

Brynjolfsson and his team started with a detailed survey, looking at the business practices and IT investments of 179 big US companies, and followed this up with interviews.

The results were clear cut.

Companies that emphasised data and analytics showed output and productivity that was 5 per cent to 6 per cent higher than their peers.

There were similar differences in other performance measures, such as asset utilisation, return on equity and market value. And the researchers used careful statistical checks to rule out reverse causality – the possibility that the productivity gains had led to the emphasis on data-driven decision-making, rather than the other way round.

Though a productivity gain of one in 20 may not seem huge,

it's worth remembering that this was, in each case, across the entire company. Brynjolfsson sees this as just the first evidence of a gathering trend. And, as he says, a 5 per cent increase in productivity is quite enough to separate the winners from the losers in most industries.

If you get an extra car off the production line for every 20 you make, that's a lot of cars by the end of the year.

Within a marketing operation, with less repetitive routine and more decisions to be made, it is hard to imagine that the gains conferred by using data and analytics would not be a good deal higher than that 5 per cent or so.

During my own career, I have often seen companies increase their profits by up to 20 per cent over the first three years of using analytics.

The more traditional academic support for the idea goes back a long way. Francis Bacon, of course, was supposed to have said 'Knowledge itself is power' round about 1600. The pioneering statistician David Blackwell looked at how better information improved payoffs in decision-making, in 1953, and concluded that improved information always improves performance. Jay R Galbraith, twenty years later, drew attention to the need for more information as tasks became more complex.

But the other influential recent study of the impact of analytics was published in 2010 in the MIT Sloan Management Review, in an article by Steve LaValle and others. This found that organisations using business information and analytics to differentiate themselves within their industries were twice as likely as others to be top performers.

These companies 'put analytics to use in the widest possible range of decisions, large and small' and made decisions based on rigorous analysis at more than twice the rate of lower performers.

They were twice as likely to use analytics to shape future strategies (the traditional role of business analytics), but also twice as likely to use insights from analytics to guide day-to-day operations.

This last observation could be the most important of the lot. Grand strategy is obviously important, but day-to-day decision-making is where the rubber meets the road. This is where analytics can most directly improve the performance of every company, if it can be made available to ordinary non-specialists in packages that can be used on ordinary PCs and laptops.

* * * * *

Every marketing department has big decisions that it needs to take, and get right, a few times a year. It also has hundreds, possibly thousands, of small, relatively mundane decisions to make every year that don't receive the same kind of deliberation and debate.

Yet, at present, there is seldom enough relevant and usable information to hand to make either the big or the small decisions a matter of rational choice.

As a result, rather than rational marketing, we have marketing departments driven mainly by what Erik Brynjolfsson called 'experience and intuition' and by the unhelpful group dynamics that surface when uncertainty meets a lack of information.

As more researchers focus on these issues, the evidence is becoming increasingly clear. A recent blog for the Harvard Business Review by Patrick Spenner and Anna Bird of the Corporate Executive Board reported on a study of 800 big company marketers which found 'the vast majority' still relied too much on intuition.

Spenner and Bird were clearly taken aback by the way assumptions ('older consumers don't use Facebook or send text messages') and 'gut-based decision making' outscored data when it came to influencing the behaviour of individual marketers.

'On average,' they claimed, 'marketers depend on data for just 11 per cent of all customer-related decisions.'

But there's no such thing as safety in numbers, either. Groups often make poor decisions. The forces at work within a department generate a pressure towards three undesirable tendencies – conformity, behavioural cascades (like when people in the old USSR would see a queue forming outside a shop and immediately join it, on the assumption that there must be something there to buy) and group polarisation.

Without external sources of objective information, conformity is a major characteristic of group behaviour. People sit on their hands if they are not sure. They back off from contradicting their bosses. Even if their instinct is to disagree, they think: 'This isn't worth it. I'm not dying in a ditch for this. I'm going to choose the battles I fight.'

This means that the presence of just one confident, consistent, unwavering voice can often decide an issue for a whole group, even if most of the members are doubtful about the decision. The apparent strength of the personality is implicitly transferred to the argument he or she is putting forward, even if the speaker has no coercive power and no special expertise or knowledge. Even, in fact, if the speaker is totally wrong.

Emotions and motivation also push people towards conformity. Individuals are more likely to conform if a task is difficult or if they are frightened. An interesting study by Robert Baron of the University of Iowa showed that conformity *decreases* if people stand to make money from a decision, as long as the task is easy. On the other hand, if they have money riding on it but the task is difficult, their behaviour lurches through 180 degrees and their willingness to conform *increases* dramatically.

So if bonuses depend on the marketing team getting the right answer and the problem facing you is highly complex, conformity rules and a consensus is all too readily achieved. What's worse, there is evidence that those facing this kind of difficult or ambiguous problem will not just agree with each other, but do so with heightened confidence.

One of the leading experimenters in this field, Solomon Asch, discovered in the 1950s that the size of a group of people who are proposing some obviously wrong decision or action is important.

His research found that if there were just two people and one was a plant, trying to influence the other to go along with a wrong judgment, the other person would seldom be swayed. With two stool pigeons in a group of three, the third person would be persuaded to deny the evidence of his or her senses about one time in seven.

But adding a third of these decoy ducks caused the number of nonsensical decisions to rise sharply. Outnumbered three to one, the odd man out would be sufficiently convinced to conform and go along with the others more than 30 per cent of the time. Adding even more people, Asch found, made no further difference, though later studies have cast doubt on this and tended to show that continuing to increase group size does increase the pressure to conform.

All this is interesting, and may ring bells for some marketers.

One consolation, though, is Asch's observation that both conformity and the acceptance of error were dramatically reduced throughout the group if there was just one sane, dissenting voice. The story of the emperor's new clothes clearly has some relevance to debates in marketing departments.

Behavioural cascades are more complicated. They occur because of people blindly following the crowd and failing to rely on or disclose their own private information. This information that's suppressed could be factual, or it might just be a qualm about what is being suggested, or a vague memory of something similar that went horribly wrong at some time in the past.

Cascades – I tend to think of them more as snowballing, really, though they can often build up until a major avalanche occurs – happen everywhere. They certainly take place in marketing departments.

These cascades often begin quietly enough. Someone gets convinced about something and manages to persuade one or two others to subscribe to the idea. When others arrive on the scene – maybe newcomers joining the department – they tend to go along with what appears to be accepted fact. In the absence of hard evidence, other people's behaviour seems like useful information, and the cascade grows.

It is important to recognise that all that is needed to set the ball rolling is one misguided person and one or two mindless (or, at least, uncritical) followers. Those who come along later are not necessarily mindless. They join the cascade because they see before them what looks like evidence. Other people seem to think this is right, so they mistakenly use the behaviour of their colleagues as information, and it may well be the only information they have to go on.

This is how myths are formed and handed down. This is how raindance rituals develop, often originating in just one person's prejudices or assumptions. Someone leaps to a conclusion about a causal connection between A and B, between a certain type of campaign and a sales upturn, and the basis for a raindance is established, enshrined in a myth that is passed down in the culture of the department.

Cascades can be particularly subtle and dangerous. In conformity situations, the conforming person who keeps quiet to avoid crossing the boss or out of solidarity with the peer group doesn't necessarily swallow the myth. But the person caught up in the cascade does – and is likely to defend it stoutly.

The problem with cascades is that once they get going, they have a life and momentum of their own. Beliefs become part of the folklore and even if more information comes in, it is not necessarily enough to disrupt the raindance. It takes powerful and striking evidence to persuade people to discard beliefs that have been in place within a company for several years.

Because of this, it would make a lot of sense to arrange bonus schemes and incentives in the marketing department to reward people for revealing information and opinions to the group, even in the form of disagreement and dissent. The other side of this coin is the removal of disincentives for revealing information, even if it is likely to be unpopular. (The extreme case of this is the company that actively encourages whistleblowers.)

In his book, *Why Societies Need Dissent*, Cass Sunstein of the University of Chicago even goes so far as to suggest that companies might want to have two rival groups working on the same problem, simply to increase the likelihood of all the possible information being revealed. That flies in the face of today's standard business practice, but it was the approach that was successfully used, for example, during the breakneck rush to develop airborne radar systems in the darkest days of World War II.

The third unhelpful group dynamic, group polarisation, is the universal tendency of groups, as a whole, to take up more extreme positions than their members would take as individuals.

Ask members of the marketing team whether television or radio would be a better bet for a product in a particular market and they will reveal a range of opinions, maybe tending on balance towards television. Put the team together in the same room to discuss the question and the group's view will harden. By the time it's all over, the decision will come out far more decisively in favour of a TV campaign than any individual would really have wanted.

With all these factors pushing groups of colleagues towards uncritical consensus, it might seem that the ideal marketing team would be made up of people who don't like each other. It doesn't work like that, though. Personal conflicts can be shown to lead to bad performance. The ideal answer, according to research led by Karen Jehn of the Wharton School in the mid-1990s, would be to put together a team composed of individuals with widely varied backgrounds and experience, each ready to stand up for his or her views, prepared and even encouraged to disagree with each other, but sharing a common set of values.

Other tips from the academics include formally assigning someone in the group to the role of devil's advocate, and bringing in experts who are not directly involved, so that they can challenge prevailing dogma.

All these insights and techniques are concerned with counteracting the predictable weaknesses of marketing teams that are forced to operate without the benefit of the objective facts that modelling and other analytics can bring to the discussion.

But even if it were possible to draw out every scrap of information and experience from the individuals in the marketing team and avoid the triple danger of conformity, cascades and polarisation, there would still be plenty of scope for modelling to add a valuable extra dimension.

* * * * *

What modelling brings is more than just that awkward voice in the corner.

Apart from breaking down the rituals and habits I have referred to as raindances, it introduces genuinely fresh new ideas and perspectives. It draws on forms of data that individuals cannot hold and manipulate in their heads, and it throws up correlations and potential causal connections that would not occur to human observers.

In most cases, a previously unimagined correlation will be coincidence, a statistical freak that can be dismissed immediately when it is brought to the marketer's notice. Occasionally, however, an emerging pattern or the sight of two lines twitching in unison will be the clue to something new and valuable, a glimpse of an insight that nobody has had before.

More often, of course, modelling plays the equally important role of discrediting and demolishing pet theories and assumptions that have become woven into the raindance culture. We see accepted truths within the marketing department held up to scrutiny in the light of the factual evidence, with modelling cast as the bringer of bad news.

But this is one of those classic cases where shooting the messenger is a big mistake. The messages modelling brings need to be heard. Their implications may be provisional and must always be subject to checking against common sense and experience, but their objectivity adds an important element to the mix.

It's worth remembering, though, that it's not the marketers' fault that they have generally had to operate without the benefit of proper information.

Much traditional marketing is inevitably based on the observation of what has happened in other companies. Take the four case studies of Institute of Practitioners in Advertising Effectiveness Award winners included in this book. They are there because they are likely to be interesting and stimulating to marketers who face similar situations and can draw parallels between the award winners and their own organisations. But companies, markets, products and business environments are so varied and change so rapidly that these tales from the coalface are only ever going to be valuable as hints and tips and food for thought. They can suggest approaches and ways of thinking, but they can't provide answers to your company's specific problems.

With modelling, it's different. You are dealing with insights and possible explanations based on subsets of a particular company's own data for a specific product or region. This is bottom-up hypothesis, looking for a story to fit the marketer's own facts, rather than top-down theorising, looking for a handful of facts to fit a preconceived notion.

This ability to bring locally specific data to bear on marketing decisions is a key factor in dislodging raindancing myths. And that's important, because the traditions and habits that grow up within a marketing department can be extraordinarily persistent.

When this kind of group has made up its mind about something, even on a split points decision, researchers have found that the result gets very firmly internalised. A classic series of pre-war experiments by psychologist Muzafer Sherif showed that group members would cling tenaciously to the point of view that had been adopted, as if it were a truth that they, as individuals, had established for themselves. A year later, Sherif's study showed, people were still fiercely defending such decisions and even trotting them out as their own ideas.

If someone says 'You know what? It was this campaign that did that – I know it for certain', and everyone else nods and agrees, this view will easily pass into departmental folklore.

Once it's embedded like this in the department's thinking, this folk wisdom will often persist for years, handed down unchallenged from generation to generation as people move on and new members join the group – even when all the original members have gone.

Marketing departments tend to be fairly hierarchical and, like most other groups, quite conservative. Once a practice or belief has become established, it is likely to be perpetuated until such time as it is seen to be causing serious problems.

Even then, if there is any uncertainty about what is causing the difficulties, people will usually stick to what they've always done. In the general course of events within a marketing group, no new data is likely to appear that will categorically destroy a long-established myth once and for all.

So unless you decide to do some proper modelling, there won't be one single dramatic insight or factual revelation that will highlight the fact that TV doesn't work for your products or that you have always set your prices too low.

Mythbusting and pattern-breaking are important benefits of introducing desktop analytics and modelling into the marketing environment. But the factual, objective nature of the data-based approach has subtler side effects that are less obvious. It pushes the marketing department towards operating in a less hierarchical, more meritocratic way, giving talented individuals more opportunity to come through and make their mark. And it can help marketers stand up for themselves in the corporate environment, where their discipline is often seen as a set of soft skills, a luxury compared with the gritty realities of production, sales and finance. When it comes to defending a marketing budget, there is nothing so powerful as being able to prove that even a small cut is going to make a big dent in the bottom line.

I said, at the beginning of this chapter, that I believe in rationality. I do. In marketing terms, trusting everything to intuition and waiting for luck or coincidence to favour your efforts seems to me no better than doing a raindance and hoping for the best. Planning future activities without knowing what numbers you can reasonably expect is simply negligent. Now that we have the tools available to make rational marketing a practical reality, there is really no excuse for pinning your faith on miracles.

'Nothing is more difficult, and therefore more precious,
than to be able to decide'
– Napoleon

CHAPTER 3

What Do Marketers Do?

Marketing is about placing your bets, and it's crazy to ignore form. Modelling plus judgment is the key breakthrough. The prize? Maybe 3 per cent to 8 per cent higher sales, just through optimising marketing spending.

What is it that marketers actually try to do? What is the essence of their position? When you look at it closely, the job has quite a lot of parallels with other, apparently unrelated roles, like that of the stock market investor.

In practice, what the marketer has to do is make an investment into a vehicle – an advertising or marketing campaign – which is intended to increase sales of a product and thus bring in a positive return. The art lies in choosing the right vehicle. In the same way, the investor or fund manager has to choose the right class of asset (equities, bonds, gold, property, maybe Rembrandts) and then pick the right individual asset within that class to maximise the return.

Like investors, marketers make their living by placing their bets. Improving marketing effectiveness revolves around improving the ability to place those bets at the right time, in the right place.

In the stock market, the question is first whether the risk/reward characteristics of the asset class are what you are looking for and then whether the individual company or commodity is going to perform as you expect. The parallel with marketing is close.

But if the problem is simple – where to place your bets – the solution is not nearly so clear cut.

You just have to look around to see the limitations that affect these decisions at the moment. Most marketing decisions are, quite frankly, a shot in the dark, informed not by evidence but by the experience of the most senior marketer involved.

It's probably safe to assume that this approach will not deliver the ultimate in optimised effectiveness or generate the best possible results. That is tacitly accepted, everywhere, so all marketing successes tend to be judged in relative, rather than absolute, terms.

One of the tantalising questions, then, is how much we are missing.

To put it another way, how great would the benefits be if we could move beyond this hit-and-miss approach and get much closer to a theoretically perfect level of marketing effectiveness?

What would the paybacks be, if we started to get it right? How big could that prize be?

My own back-of-the-envelope calculations – based on the gaps I have seen in big companies between what the companies actually do and what would seem to be available to them if they pursued optimised strategies – indicate that the sums involved could often run into the millions. Across UK business as a whole, it would be several billions. In the US economy, the numbers could be astronomical.

In my experience, individual companies can typically increase sales revenues by 3 per cent to 8 per cent and boost profits by up to 20 per cent over the medium term, just by optimising their marketing investments.

It is hard to think of any other change a company could make that could create such immediate and profitable leverage.

But business is remarkably conservative. People need a lot of convincing. And they are especially reluctant to take any step that smacks of handing over decision-making power. We all tend to believe that we make better decisions than other people, and certainly much better than any little PC software package is going to come up with.

This is unfortunate, for two reasons. Assuming the experts who have been involved in developing the package really know their stuff, there is every reason to believe that the wisdom and experience embedded in a serious piece of business software might amount to more than most of us as individuals could muster. And secondly, human beings are unavoidably prone to bias, prejudice and error.

Way back in the 1950s, Professor Paul Meehl of the University of Minnesota conducted a classic study of doctors and how well they performed at diagnosing diseases and other conditions on first presentation. They were pitted against automated statistical systems based on diagnostic programs, and the machines won hands down. Time and again, it was shown that even the fairly primitive systems of the day outscored the doctors in correctly identifying what was wrong with the patient.

That wasn't the result the doctors expected or wanted to see. It wasn't even the result patients would necessarily have wanted, as there is potentially a lot of value in face-to-face contact with a doctor, quite apart from the delivery of an accurate diagnosis. But diagnosis is generally the key to solving health problems. It's the fork in the road. Get it wrong and everything that follows will be wrong.

Human beings are fallible. Even doctors. They make mistakes that statistically-based automated systems don't make. And there are certain specific types of problem or challenge that tend to bring out the worst in all of us, including doctors.

Economist Terrance Odean ran a long series of studies on the issue of overconfidence and discovered that lawyers, engineers, chief executives and investment bankers, as well as doctors, all thought they knew a lot more than they really did.

But all humans – not just these highly-paid experts – appear to be consistently bad at applying their judgment to complex situations. The more complex the issue at hand, the more certain we tend to be that we are right. Yet, for all the obvious reasons, the reverse is true. As the cases we're examining become more complicated, we actually make worse decisions and think we're making better ones.

Since the issue of resource allocation – placing your bets – in today's complex and fragmented media and business world is the key question for marketers, industry faces a real problem here.

There is an urgent need for techniques, technologies and solutions that will make sense of this dizzying, overwhelming, judgment-exhausting complexity and give us evidence-based explanations and analysis of past performance – and robust, trustworthy forecasts and options for the future.

This is why the area that I work in is so exciting and important.

Statistical prediction can outperform people. Modelling can provide a lot of the answers that we all need. By virtue of being able to give people easy, affordable tools that can give them access to this performance and these answers, I have found myself part of a new revolution that could change the world in quite significant ways.

But although these new analysis and modelling tools can be made quick and simple enough for non-specialists to use, I am aware that some people reading this book will not want to be fobbed off with bland assurances that what we're doing is statistically sound and mathematically justifiable.

There's no easy way round this. I have one audience that is only likely to be interested in these tools in terms of their outputs and what they can do for resource allocation in business and another that will want to know exactly what's going on and why it works.

Later in the book – in Chapter 9: Talking with Martians and Chapter 10: Modelling 101 – there is quite a lot of technical detail and a fairly specific exposition of the principles, thinking and techniques that are deployed in today's marketingQED software.

By the time we get there, I hope most people will be clear enough about the basic ideas of marketing mix modelling to enjoy finding out a bit more about what goes on under the hood. If that's not for you, you could jump straight on to Chapter 11: Tales from the Front Line. But if you are at all interested in grappling with the technicalities of modern analytics and modelling, you will certainly find a lot of detail there that has simply not been written down anywhere else.

Indeed, for some people, Chapters 9 and 10, on their own,

will be a complete and ample justification for the publication of this book.

Many of the ideas that are unpacked and explored in these chapters will have been mentioned elsewhere in the book. In many cases, understanding the broad outline of what a particular concept means in the business environment is essential for an understanding of the marketing revolution we are discussing. So, for example, it's important to know about the significance of the S-curve, though it's not necessarily essential to know much about the mathematics and statistical theory that lie behind it.

The S-curve, shown in Fig 1, below, is the bane of marketers' lives. It's the curved graph, like a lazy, flattened-out S, that marks the typical pattern of response to many different kinds of marketing initiative.

Fig 1. A typical S-curve: it's all too easy to jump off too soon

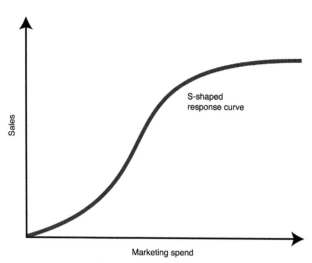

What the S-curve shows is that, at first, you tend to spend your money and see disappointingly little to show for it. Things get going slowly, and there is a stage, sometimes agonisingly long, when the money is going out and there is very little sign of a corresponding build-up of consumer response in terms of sales. All being well, this phase ends and the response curve starts to climb steeply, ideally in a nicely predictable way, so that the more resources you put in, the more response you get out.

As a marketer, you want this phase to go on as long as possible. But eventually it will end. And it will end by flattening out again, at the top of the S, as you start to enter the realm of diminishing returns, where you are getting less and less extra response for each additional unit of cash or effort you put into the campaign.

In practice, I have seen any number of cases where companies have failed to maximise the profit potential of their products or services by quitting too soon when the S-curve starts to flatten out.

It is obvious that no-one is going to be overjoyed at seeing the return on each extra unit of investment start to tail off. But unless you have other projects or products you can switch your investment into and that are definitely going to deliver higher rates of return, it is often wise to continue riding the S-curve further up than gut instinct might dictate.

This is a point that is very frequently – and expensively – misunderstood by semi-numerate senior management, which may not really understand what is going on.

Back at the bottom end of the S, where it all begins, the marketer's ambition is always to shorten or eliminate the first flat segment of the curve. The Holy Grail would be to find marketing tactics and media strategies that would jolt you straight onto the steeper middle section of the S-curve, without the start-up period where time and money seem to dwindle rapidly while sales stubbornly refuse to lift off.

While we're looking at concepts like the S-curve, we must also recognise some of the fundamental limitations of the analytical approach. Modelling can't solve everything.

Even when modelling has delivered some fresh insights and seems to have put you on the right track to take firm decisions that will improve business performance, its findings and suggestions have to be sanity checked and matched against human judgment and industry knowledge.

One reason for this is the simple one that analytics is very good at showing that this varies with that and these increase as those are raised.

But what it shows, in cases like this, are correlations. And since, apart from anything else, there is a lot of coincidence in the world, correlation is not necessarily the same thing as causality. Just because two changes are simultaneous, it doesn't mean that one change directly caused the other.

Statistical analysis can give us indications of where robust correlations are present. What it cannot do is tell us, definitively, if these correlations point to a causal relationship. It may be that, over a short period one summer, the price of gold is correlated to the sales of ice creams. But no-one would believe this represented a causal relationship. The gold price does not cause the sales of ice creams. They just happen to be moving in synch for a few weeks.

This is a problem for the current way people do modelling. A mathematical model is basically an equation that connects a number of variables, based on your belief that, say, the factors that determine your sales volume are likely to be price, advertising and hours of sunshine. A model is created, usually by hand, and the correlations look good. But how do we know whether the model that has been dreamed up represents a real causal relationship or just a neat correlation?

This is actually a serious headache, because of an interesting phenomenon from the philosophy of science called *underdetermination*.

Underdetermination is the idea that a data set may be able to support multiple theories that explain the same data. The classic example of underdetermination is the two competing theories of how the planets move. The limited data available in the early part of the 16th century meant that the old theory that placed the earth at the centre of the universe was just as well supported by the facts as Copernicus' heliocentric theory. The data was not good enough to enable the scientists of the day to crown one theory the winner. New data was needed before the Copernican revolution could win the day and change the way mankind saw the world.

The way modelling has traditionally been done is flawed for much the same reason. Modelling experts would craft one model by hand that seemed to pass the statistical tests of correlation and then present it to the world as representing the truth. But making that leap from correlation to causality is not justified. Ideally, the modeller needs to generate *all* of the possible models that could fit the data and then leave the identification of the causal relationship to those who understand the market.

If this is not possible, more data is needed to add to the weight of evidence supporting a particular model. And because markets vary over time, by the time new data is analysed it may not be capable of proving which theory was right. The relationships may no longer hold. This leaves the boffin in something of a quandary.

Look at the data in the following table. The data is made up, but it will help demonstrate just how misleading it can be to only see part of the story.

Cholesterol index		Exercise levels			
		High	Moderate	Low	None
Genetic propensity for high cholesterol	High	9	11	12	13
	Average	8	10	11	12
	Low	7	9	10	11

Difference = 2

Difference = 4

The table shows an index for the levels of cholesterol in patients' blood. The different numbers show the effects on that index of a patient's genetic propensity to develop high cholesterol, on the one hand, and the patient's exercise habits, on the other. We can see that the difference in the index caused by exercise is 4 points, while the difference due to genes is only 2. We would naturally conclude from this that exercise makes twice the difference.

But suppose we were only given a portion of this data, as shown in the table below.

Cholesterol index		Exercise levels	
		Moderate	None
Genetic propensity for high cholesterol	High	11	13
	Average	10	12
	Low	9	11

Difference = 2

Difference = 2

This time our conclusion would be different. We would regard exercise and genes as having roughly the same impact on blood cholesterol, all other things being equal. Because we can't see the full picture, we are misled into accepting a result that isn't right.

The same thing can happen when trying to judge models. If you cannot see the full range of possible models that fit the data, you will not be able to judge the differences between them. This is an issue that can cause considerable difficulties. Without the full context you can easily draw false conclusions, even if you have gone to the trouble of doing some analysis.

It has been a serious problem for many years that the increasingly powerful analytical tools the boffins have developed have been suitable for use only by fellow boffins, or by consultants who have taught themselves to use them and made this kind of work their speciality.

These highly specialised consultants – and I speak from experience, as I've been one of them myself – are always going to be outsiders, to some degree. They are only brought in once or twice a year (certainly, because of the cost, no more than quarterly) and can usually only produce snapshots of what is going on. If you spent enough money, you could have them in your offices, as part of the family, on a permanent basis, and no doubt they would do a good job. But cost would generally rule that out as an option.

Inevitably, then, we have a situation where the consultants usually lack the nuanced industry knowledge of the marketers. The marketers lack the ability to handle the esoteric analytical and modelling tools the consultants use. And, even at its very best, a snapshot every six months or so is only ever going to be of limited use in informing day-to-day marketing decisions.

We all know the situation where a media company has TV time or magazine space it wants to offload in a hurry. Maybe the media owner is dangling a half-price deal in front of you, as long as you can take up the offer immediately. It's no good hoping the twice-a-year analysis will be able to give you any guidance on that snap decision. You're flying blind, back to relying on gut feel and what Erik Brynjolfsson called 'experience and intuition'. The next update may well be able to tell you, several months later, whether you got it right or wrong. But that's no help at all at the time the decision needs to be made.

After working in this field for years, the team at marketingQED eventually realised that the answer to the problems of correlation vs causality and of good information that arrives too late to be used would be to somehow make modelling and analysis as real-time as possible. We also needed to find a way to make it easy and quick for marketers to access the analysis themselves – to assess the candidate models, select the one that seems to reflect causal truth and exploit the new insights while the opportunities last.

If the marketer, sitting at a desk in the office, could use a range of smart analytical tools with the same ease and nonchalance with which he or she used PowerPoint or Excel, that would change everything.

So what we have created is a set of tools that deliver the insight needed to make decisions on a continuous basis. The software system we have developed at marketingQED creates a kind of analysis laboratory where people can generate and automatically run through many different models that seek to match and represent the real world situation that gave rise to their data from past events and past sales.

But underdetermination means there could be any number of models and combinations of factors that fitted the data for a particular company. The modelling software must generate a variety of different models that fit with and potentially explain the data, allowing the marketer to then step in and examine them to dismiss the most unlikely and identify the one that is most likely to represent reality. In my opinion, only people with an understanding of their market can pinpoint actual causal relationships from among a clutch of neat correlations.

Marketers now have a choice. They can use the tools themselves or work in partnership with internal or external consultants, who will use the tools to deliver the candidate models for the marketers to assess. The key point is that modelling can now be available on tap, at a fraction of the price it would have cost before.

The software lab we have developed to create these potential models works on Darwinian principles, using a genetic algorithm to breed thousands of models, generation on generation on generation, at very high speed.

Each element of the equation is treated like a gene and the process starts with the creation of a random population of models. These are then examined to see how well each model performs and the worst performers are killed off. Models that seem to have good qualities are bred together and a new generation of baby models emerges. The babies are ranked, the worst performers killed off, and the process goes through another cycle.

All this takes seconds. As one generation of these statistical fruit flies follows another, certain genetic traits persist and are maintained, contributing to the fitness of the models that bear them. Eventually, this process delivers a crop of models that all perform well against the data.

As far as the software is concerned, any one of these might be the real explanation of what caused a fluctuation in sales. But this is where the knowledge and skill of the marketer come into play, in tossing away pretenders that may be based on luck or coincidence and recognising the models that seem to make sense in the real world.

The great value of this approach is that all these different models can be created very quickly and that it is the people who are in the know, the people who understand the market best, who will decide which of them are likely to mean something.

The marketer will be looking at the models that appear to fit the facts best and using his or her judgment to choose the one that seems most likely to represent causal connections, rather than just correlations.

This is the breakthrough.

We know that people have blind spots and simply aren't good at interpreting large and complex data sets, while computer-based analytics is fantastically capable in this area. We know, too, that for all their number-crunching power and statistical sophistication, the systems the technicians have developed are still perfectly capable of coming up with models that look like a good fit to the data but are obviously wrong in common sense terms or in the light of reliable industry knowledge.

But bringing superhuman modelling power and human judgment together is the basis for a winning combination. And making this combination so quick and easy to use that it can be applied to imminent tactical decisions is a change with such enormous money-saving and money-making potential that it could transform the nature of the marketing role.

Humans are very smart – far smarter and faster than computers – when it comes to some aspects of numeracy. We may need a lot of calculations to tell us that the weight of a car is 1.7 tonnes, rather than 1.9. But, unlike the computer, we all of us know, instantly and unthinkingly, that the right answer is not going to be either 0.17 tonnes or 17 tonnes.

Many products sell more at Christmas. If you wanted to know whether sales of, say, champagne rose over Christmas because of your campaign or simply because of the time of year, you might need some shrewd analysis to separate out the variables and find the right answer. If you wanted to know whether sales of car tyres or tins of baked beans over the same period had responded to your marketing activity or risen simply because of seasonal factors, you probably wouldn't need a computer at all. Industry knowledge and just being human would tell you to expect no natural Christmas upswing and that any sales increase probably was reflecting something you'd done.

Giving marketing teams access to analytics and modelling packages they can use themselves, so they can apply their judgment and experience in an informed way, is capturing the best of both worlds. Until very recently, though, it was assumed that this was not practical.

Now, using the new algorithms to find suitable models and taking advantage of the enormous computing power that is available in every PC and laptop, it is perfectly possible. Within a few years, every serious marketer will have access to these new tools and the era of raindancing will be at an end.

*'When I disagree with a rational man,
I let reality be our final arbiter.
If I am right, he will learn; if I am wrong, I will'*
— *Ayn Rand*

CHAPTER 4

How it Works

How does the wisdom of crowds work? Why do dummies make a group more intelligent? Why marketing is ready to move beyond the amateur era and start spending the right budgets on the right things.

The key to removing the hit-and-miss raindancing element from marketing and replacing it with a rational approach is to make full use of the data that's available to us.

Using the statistical techniques of modelling, we can look in minute detail at a company's past sales volumes and marketing activities, examine them against relevant background factors such as competitors' campaigns, weather and seasonal influences and develop hypotheses about what was really going on.

One simple, fundamental reason why this is a good approach is the fact that it draws on a potentially vast amount of data.

You probably know about the concept of the wisdom of crowds, made fashionable a few years ago by a bestselling book of the same name by James Surowiecki. The basic idea is that if you can collect information – even information of very mixed quality – from enough people, you are likely to be able to come up with surprisingly accurate answers.

You may, for example, be able to arrive at a very good

estimated result, even if it is logically impossible for any one of your respondents to know the right answer.

The original, classic example of this was the story told by the brilliant Sir Francis Galton, cousin of Darwin and father of modern statistics, who visited a country fair and was intrigued by the stand where visitors competed to guess the weight of an ox. There were plenty of livestock experts around who might have been able to guess its actual weight, but the complication was that they were asked to guess the final weight of meat from the animal *after* the beast had been slaughtered, cut up and dressed.

Nearly 800 people recorded their guesses, and, of course, nobody got it exactly right. But Galton took all the guesses away and studied the numbers. The actual final weight, as announced by the judges, was 1,198 pounds.

Galton decided that the 'middlemost estimate' (the median) should be taken as being the opinion of the crowd, 'every other estimate being condemned as too low or too high by the majority of the voters'. This came out at 1,207 pounds, within 1 per cent of the right answer – a startling result, given that no-one really had a clue what the exact weight would be.

Galton was amazed. And he was even more astounded later when he realised that the straightforward arithmetical mean – in layman's terms, the average – was even more astonishingly accurate. Averaging out the guesses from 787 readable tickets, he found that they gave an answer of 1,197 pounds. That was not what Galton had expected, and he was certainly not looking for evidence that a random crowd could perform such a remarkable feat of collective judgment.

It underlines the point that large sample sizes always help. Given enough raw data, it is always likely that the errors within the sample will largely cancel each other out. Conceptually, that's not too hard to take. We can all accept the idea that this will happen if there is some basic core of knowledge somewhere within the sampled population.

What is more intriguing, in the case of the ox and many other instances, is how good crowds are at answering questions where nobody can possibly know the facts. In practice, it turns out that a large number of people, collectively, will almost always come up with a better answer than a small group – even if that group is made up of handpicked (or elected) sages.

In general, any approach that enables you to utilise the information from a very large data source has the potential to deliver knowledge and insight. Even simple sales records can be seen, cumulatively, as messages from the markets.

What an individual consumer buys, where and when, and how the payment is made, may or may not provide useful information. Everyone buys milk, so the individual transaction may not mean much. But if someone buys a ready meal for one in a supermarket at 12.30 at night, it may imply a lot about that person's social and domestic arrangements. Multiply this data up by millions and there is clearly plenty of detail to be discovered.

Analytics can do this. Modelling unlocks information hidden in the data that the marketer can't ordinarily see.

The sheer number of data points is a benefit in itself. In a marketing department, there will usually be bright people with many different points of view. There will be product managers around, media specialists, creative teams and other agency people, all chipping in and feeding their ideas into the mix. But that is still a fairly small community, and one in which group thinking, common assumptions and established raindancing habits are likely to play a big part.

Think of new product launches. Every year there are thousands upon thousands of product launches, from companies large and small. Most of them fail. Not just most, but almost all. Yet every one of those new products must surely have been conceived, developed, tested and marketed by people who thought it was likely to succeed.

There is a mass of research evidence that explains why small groups get product launches, advertising campaigns and all kinds of other projects wrong.

This is a hobbyhorse of mine, so I'll have to resist the temptation to mention all the interesting findings. But there was a fascinating study carried out at the University of Michigan, for example, that showed that diversity within groups was essential – to the point where a group that included a few dummies (not the experimenter's exact words, I admit) would consistently make better decisions than a group made up entirely of smart guys.

More evidence in support of the benefits of diversity came from one of America's leading organisational theorists, Professor James G March of Stanford University, who looked at how difficult it was for any established group to keep on learning. March recommended the deliberate introduction of a leavening of dummies, too. (I can see a new, potentially popular, book taking shape here, maybe called *Dummies for Dummies*.) These non-experts come at an issue from different directions, ask new – sometimes daft – questions and force the experts to re-examine their assumptions. March came to the conclusion that the continuing development of knowledge within a group depends on 'maintaining an influx of the naïve and ignorant'.

Homogeneous groups, March said, find it hard to keep learning, because each member is bringing less and less new information to the table. As a result, unmixed groups spend too much time exploiting and not enough time exploring.

Diversity in decision-making groups helps to break up biases and unchallenged consensus. But the best antidote to groupthink is the injection of new and objective information. And modelling introduces new information in a processed form that allows insights, or at least hypotheses, to be explored and discussed.

This is a situation that does suit the group's strengths. The information is fresh and the modelling will usually have produced more than one hypothetical explanation that might account for the sales or other results that are being examined. There is a vital role here for the experience and expertise within the marketing group, as some of the hypotheses thrown up by the model will need to be weeded out as nonsensical.

Modelling, after all, is a matter of identifying and highlighting correlations. The model cannot begin to say whether A caused B, or even whether B caused A. At the same time, all the hypotheses that the modelling presents will share one valuable attribute. They will all be consistent with the data, which is not always the case with the hypotheses dreamed up by marketers under more traditional circumstances.

Throughout the raindancing era, while marketing has had to operate without any substantial decision support mechanisms, guesswork and hopeful theorising have been the order of the day. If you have no other weapons in your armoury, gut feel, experience and other people's anecdotes are all you can draw on.

Most marketers have had a very limited information set to work with. They have usually had aggregated records of past sales, month by month or week by week and region by region. They have had details of budgets and production and media costs. They have had market reports that have given them some inkling of where their products fit in among their competitors. And they have had qualitative survey results and focus groups.

Using just this sketchy collection of raw materials, they have tried to build a narrative and interpret what has happened in the past, what is going on in the present and what may be expected in the future.

Testing of new marketing ideas would usually be on a suck-it-and-see basis, involving actually carrying out trials. Regional trial launches, split tests for creative executions and other trials and pilot projects would all take time and resources and often deliver disappointing or unclear results. But much of the information that might have been gleaned from a regional trial, for example, could potentially be derived from clever modelling.

These days, of course, the combination of effectively unlimited computing power, the online business environment and advanced analytic techniques has changed the face of marketing for those who are happily positioned to take advantage of it.

At Amazon, for example, when the marketers wanted to test out different price points for books, they were able to try offering the same book at different prices to different people and measure the precise differences in response.

You may remember the furious row that broke out when this experiment was revealed.

Customers were convinced that they were being unfairly overcharged for the books they bought – or that they were being discriminated against on the basis of demographics, geography or past buying record. In fact, nothing of the sort was going on. The company had tested the differential pricing on a purely random basis. Once they had harvested the price sensitivity information they were looking for, Amazon's marketers used refunds to ensure that everyone who had bought the books paid the lowest price, so nobody was actually disadvantaged.

What Amazon was doing here was setting up a laboratory-style experiment, testing a range of scenarios, building a dataset and then using analytics to figure out exactly what all the results meant. Instead of assuming it knew, intuitively, how people would respond to tiny pricing differences, it collected and collated a very large number of data points and then built a set of durable, robust hypotheses about when, where and how much price would influence book sales. As authors and customers, we see the results of this now in the weeks after a book is first published, with Amazon's price changing virtually day by day, driven by the company's powerful analytical engines.

Most companies don't have Amazon's enviable dominance of its marketplace and generally good reputation for keeping its promises. Unless they, too, operate entirely online, they are likely to have far less detailed records of every aspect of customer transactions. But every company that keeps track of its sales, its pricing, its distribution and its marketing campaigns will hold a body of data that can potentially form the basis for useful modelling exercises.

Even if nobody in the marketing department is in any doubt about what has worked in the past and why, modelling's ability to extrapolate trends and deliver accurate, quantified forecasts for the future is a game-changer.

Prediction has always, necessarily, been a matter of

guesswork. But where have those guesses come from? Unless they were completely random, which would also make them completely useless, they must have been based on some implicit calculation, which can only have been rooted in past results.

This kind of calculation is basically a rule-of-thumb estimate and is highly unlikely to take account of more than a couple of variables. Indeed, the experienced marketing director or CMO who pronounces 'I reckon we'll sell 600,000 units next year' is probably not even consciously doing the sums.

Modelling makes the mathematics of the calculation explicit and transparent.

Marketers can see, in advance, what factors are likely to affect future performance. They can see where the real sensitivities are and conduct what-if? tests to explore the impact of different strategies. They can also, for the first time, produce budget proposals grounded in reality and built on a basis of fact.

The ability to do all these things within the marketing department, whenever they are needed and with almost instant results, substantially changes the nature of marketing activity. Even in small to medium-sized firms, the introduction of desktop modelling software represents the opportunity to professionalise a sphere of activity that has often been seen by outsiders as essentially the preserve of the amateur.

This is a significant and radical change. Rational marketing has implications that extend far beyond the marketing department itself. For example, there is no genuine logic to support the almost universal practice of handing down a fixed budget to the marketing department and telling the marketers to get on and make the best of it.

The myths and traditions that drive budget-setting are

among the most flagrant examples of raindancing.

There could hardly be anything more perversely illogical than the common habit of calculating marketing budgets as a percentage of sales. Why should 10 per cent of sales revenue be the right figure? By what logic? Marketing's job is to cause sales, not reflect them. If I had no sales, I would do some marketing to change that situation. But by this logic, I'd be given no marketing budget to do it with.

It is similarly crazy to set marketing budgets with reference to competitors' spending, or – and this passes for sophistication in some quarters – with reference to SOM/SOV (the share of market to share of voice ratio). That might lead you to the right budget figure, but if it did it would only be coincidence.

Let's take an extreme example. If you spend more money than everyone else in your market, your SOV is obviously high. If your market share at this point is low, your SOM/SOV ratio may look strange and oddly out of kilter with your competitors. But it just doesn't matter. What matters is simply the marginal profit you get for marginal spend. Even if you are spending twice as much as the competition, the only point to watch is whether that spending is profitable for you. If it is, SOM/SOV is profoundly irrelevant as a guide to the right budget.

The right amount to spend on a particular brand at a particular time can be deduced from examining the relevant response curve. I will have plenty more to say about that later, but the point is that it is not really a matter of opinion.

The right amount to spend on a range of products is the sum of the right amounts for the individual products. The CEO or finance director who says 'You've got £2 million this year and that's your lot' is wilfully ignoring the facts. Unless £2 million happens, just by chance, to be the right amount, the company is either going to be paying for campaigns that can no longer justify their costs or leaving profits on the table that were there for the taking.

These can be very expensive mistakes, and they are not, in this instance, marketing's fault. Though the advent of desktop marketing mix modelling will have its most obvious impact within the marketing department, there are implications that will reverberate right through to the boardroom.

'The whole is more than the sum of its parts'
– Aristotle

CHAPTER 5

Best of Both Worlds: the QED Quadrant

There's more marketing mix modelling to be done than there are rocket scientists to go round. But give marketers the tools to create their own models and forecasts, using their own data, and everything changes for the better.

For most people faced with planning marketing strategies and budgets, the idea of having access to forecasts you could trust has always been an impossible dream.

In the past, the alternatives have been getting marketing and subject experts to produce predictions based on a necessarily small data set or shipping out the full data set to outside analysts who know a lot about statistics, but often don't know about your business.

Imagine a quadrant, as in Fig 2. The horizontal axis represents detailed knowledge of your business, products and markets – we'll call that Industry Knowledge. The vertical axis represents the Quantity and Quality of Data to be evaluated. This is what I call the QED Quadrant. On the grid formed by these two axes, the best possible place to be would obviously be top right, where the maximum amount of data can be interpreted in the light of the maximum degree of industry knowledge. This is the only part of the quadrant where hit-and-miss trial and error can be replaced by the context-sensitive, data-driven reliability of rational marketing.

Fig 2. The QED Quadrant: where analytics meets insider knowhow

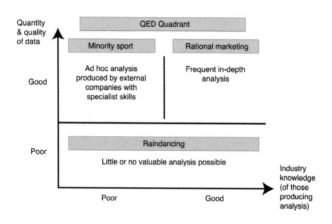

Up to now, there's never been a way to get the best of both worlds. If you wanted sophisticated analysis of a huge data set, you had to outsource the job to the external consultancies who employed the statistical rocket scientists. It wasn't quick or cheap. You couldn't afford to do it often enough, and you certainly couldn't afford to run a lot of whimsical what-if? simulations to help in planning your future budgets and activities. This approach has only ever been available for the biggest brands in the biggest countries. The vast majority of brands in most countries of the world simply can't justify the cost of doing things this way. As a result, most brands, in most places, simply don't do any modelling at all.

But once marketers have access to a vast amount of statistical and modelling expertise built into the modules of a software package that they themselves can run on ordinary office PCs or laptops, the rules of the game are changed for ever. The top right of the QED Quadrant is no longer a no-go area. Anyone can analyse, reanalyse and segment past performance, factor by factor, and generate robust, accurate simulations and predictions.

Thirty or forty years ago, marketing people had no choice. Marketers would have been stuck in the bottom half of this QED Quadrant, relying on gut feel, with virtually no large-scale data to work from. Maybe they were getting computer printouts of their aggregated sales numbers, but nothing more than that.

Experience was highly valued, because experience was all they had. But maybe the calculations were simpler. Certainly the number of marketing vehicles and media available in the UK was much more limited – one commercial TV channel, a handful of radio stations from 1973 onwards, newspapers and magazines (though far fewer than now), direct mail and outdoor. That was it. And no internet, of course.

There were fewer choices, but the lack of data and the forced reliance on the marketing guru's gut instincts meant it was probably easier to get things badly wrong. Direct mail was the one medium that offered real, solid facts you could hang your hat on, and that was only thought of as suitable for certain types of product. So people were largely flying blind. Raindancing was in fashion, because there was no alternative. Marketers would spend their time looking at what seemed to work one year, replicating it the next and being caught completely on the hop whenever changing circumstances meant that the formula needed to change.

Through the 1980s, more data was becoming available and basic computing gradually began to arrive in ordinary offices. But in the early to middle 1990s, there was an abrupt change of gear.

Suddenly you had proper, powerful PCs on most desktops, with non-specialist business tools like spreadsheets coming into general use, far more data being collected and manipulated and, of course, the coming of the internet. Marketing became more complex and fragmented, with the proliferation of different media, including multi-channel cable and satellite TV, as well as the wholly new online media.

At this point, there was no shortage of data, but most people were not at all sure what to do with it. That was something we recognised quite explicitly. We could see that the marketing teams possessed the industry knowledge but not the analytical skill set, and that this was the big opportunity. People just didn't have access to the statistical and analytical skills they would need to make sense of the data that was now flooding in on them.

Even now, there aren't all that many mathematicians around, and this kind of work would only ever attract a small subset of them. The London School of Economics Masters course in econometrics (a common type of modelling) is one of the best and most sought-after specialist courses in Europe. But that turns out just a few dozen students a year. Other universities offer superficial introductions to the subject – there's an econometrics option in most undergraduate economics courses – but those don't equip you for a career in business.

What's more, students usually try to avoid taking this option, because it's hard work. And I'm not sure anyone would claim it is anything more than a good basic grounding. You'd need to go a lot further to be able to handle modelling at the sort of level we're talking about, and you'd still need to learn a lot more about the subject during your first few years on the job.

There are only a few courses anywhere that really seem to set out to cover the practical aspects of our sort of analysis and modelling for business. There is a good Master of Science in Marketing Analysis course at the University of Ghent in Belgium that's been going for more than ten years. But apart from that, and a newer course at Lancaster University, there are few sources of potential recruits.

For the foreseeable future, there is going to be a lot more marketing mix modelling to be done than could ever be handled by this meagre supply of university-trained modellers. With hardly any companies today genuinely optimising the effectiveness of their marketing spend – and then only, as a rule, by pure coincidence – it is imperative that usable modelling and forecasting tools are made available to front-line marketers.

Perfection may be unattainable, but, even short of that, there is room for huge improvements. The money that is wasted every year by big companies failing to optimise their investment – usually by underspending – is incalculable. The total across all businesses, large and small, must certainly run into billions. If the introduction of desktop modelling software can introduce even a small element of rational marketing and a modest shift towards the top right of the QED Quadrant, it will have had a revolutionary impact.

*'The truth is often unpopular and
the contest between agreeable fancy
and disagreeable fact is unequal'*
– Adlai Stevenson

CHAPTER 6

Who Wants to See Some Film About Baseball?

Why a 2011 Brad Pitt movie about baseball should be required viewing for every marketer. It's the true story of the team that moved from wishing and hoping to looking at the numbers – and acting on them.

Moneyball is an American movie about baseball, produced by and starring Brad Pitt. When I last looked, it had taken $75 million at the box office in the US, $1.1 million in Britain and $1,900 in Ghana, where, I suppose, there is little interest in the sport.

Brad won't be too worried, though. The statistics that matter are in his favour – budget of $50 million, world take after the first six months, $110 million. That's good business, by any measure.

I'm no baseball fan myself, but the reason I sat and wrote spidery notes on a pad in the dark of an almost empty London cinema is that *Moneyball* is specifically about statistics in baseball – and I am a statistician. The film is based on the book of the same name, written in 2003 by an author called Michael Lewis, who spotted the interesting story that lay behind the sudden and phenomenal success of the underfunded and unfancied Oakland Athletics baseball team.

The Oakland A's had started the 2002 season badly, having just lost three of their star players to richer clubs. After struggling through a succession of defeats and losing a couple of the few remaining players who might have been able to turn their fortunes round, the A's suddenly started winning. And once they'd started, they didn't know how to stop. Victory followed victory until they had broken all records and compiled major league baseball's longest-ever winning streak of 20 consecutive games.

What had transformed the situation, and attracted my interest and that of Premier League football clubs, the England cricket team and many others in the UK with little direct involvement in baseball, was one crucial decision by the Oakland A's general manager, Billy Beane. When conventional methods had left his team in a slump, he had made up his mind to take crucial hire and fire decisions based on a platform of statistical information about player performance.

No longer were players to be taken on just because they had a beautiful swing, or because every now and again they would connect with a huge hit and loft the ball way up into the crowd for a spectacular home run. The accumulated wisdom, hunches and prejudices of generations of coaches, scouts, commentators, fans and ex-players were discarded in favour of 'on-base percentages' and other objective metrics.

When a big player went elsewhere, instead of trying to replace his charismatic slugging, Beane and his staff would comb the statistics to identify unglamorous and undervalued players who consistently delivered better than average on-base percentages – getting safely onto a base relatively often compared with the number of times they came to bat.

The players the stats pointed to might be old, ungainly, hampered by past injuries and emotional traumas or blessed with eccentric technique. So much the better. Beane's ability to pick up the players he needed cheaply was aided by other managers' strong preferences for tall, athletic, granite-jawed hero figures – a 'good body' or even a 'good face' – who looked the part, even though they might not often deliver.

Baseball is about scoring more runs than the other team. And runs are not only produced by big hitters. There was the fat boy whose sluggish, vulnerable body got predatory pitchers so over-excited that they pitched one 'ball' after another (the equivalent of a 'wide' in cricket, though the batter has to resist the temptation to swing at it). Four of these illegal balls and the fat boy gets a free walk to first base. The knack of inducing balls by tempting pitchers into trying too hard and losing accuracy had never been seen as a major skill for batters. Nobody put a value on it. It seemed almost invisible, probably because drawing a walk like this does not improve a player's batting average. But suddenly Billy Beane was making factors like this count and using them to make selection decisions based on players' actual performance records, rather than their reputations.

There was a point in the Oakland Athletics story where Billy Beane, as general manager, was seriously considering firing the entire coaching and scouting staff of former players and taking every decision about investments in players and team selection entirely on the basis of what his Yale-educated statistician's laptop told him.

This caught my attention, because it seemed to raise some

interesting parallels with my long struggle to bring statistical analysis to bear on the discipline of marketing.

It took as its first assumption the belief that past performance is invariably the only evidence we have on which to base predictions about the future.

For the baseball insiders, with their hunches and dreams, their dislike of skinny little guys and fat catchers, their belief in their own ability to sniff out the inner character and deeper potential of the stars of tomorrow, this was no basis for signing a player. When Billy Beane and his allies first tried to use the statistical approach to find the players needed to plug the gaps left by departing stars, it was derided as 'performance scouting' – anything but a compliment in baseball terms.

But what else is there?

Inside baseball, or marketing, or anywhere else in life, what have we got to base our forecasts on other than evidence from the past?

It may be a question of what data you choose, how much of it you use, and what weightings are given to the elements of your calculation, but all predictions are based on past experience.

Even the baseball sages and former players based their belief in a good body or a good face on what they thought they'd observed throughout their careers. When heroic-looking players pulled off heroic feats, it stuck in their minds and seemed to validate their assumptions. When the heroes failed, or the ugly mis-shapes made a winning contribution, it clashed with the assumptions and was soon forgotten, leaving the myths untarnished.

What I saw, in the first ten or fifteen years of my own career in business, was plenty of evidence that experience was, at best, a double-edged sword.

I saw folk memories and rules of thumb being elevated to the status of absolute imperatives. I met sales directors who were convinced they could tell you the optimum size for a sales force in a particular market before they knew anything about the area, the distances involved or the demographics of the region. I listened to marketing directors who just *knew* that radio commercials or outdoor or trade press advertising would not work for their products or their customers.

These people were basing their views on facts, in a sense. But they were extrapolating violently from a relatively small number of instances.

Their own limited stocks of past experiences were taken as typical of the way the world would always be. They were absorbed and remembered, unexamined for special circumstances or one-off factors that might have applied at the time. It's no great breakthrough to realise that a sample size of a few dozen ad campaigns or sales force performance in a few territories over a decade or two does not give you a multitude of data points. There is safety in numbers, if they are handled right. If you can correlate relevant data from many, many instances, you are very much more likely to be able to make consistently useful forecasts.

Billy Beane and his baseball revolution depended on generalising from a large body of evidence, rather than a small one. They used data about each player that would cover hundreds of times at bat. They assigned cash values to proven abilities, like the ability to draw 'balls' and get that free walk to first base. And because other teams didn't attach the same importance to the on-base percentages and walks the Oakland A's were looking for, Beane was able to pick up proven talents at unfashionably low prices.

The Oakland A's had started by looking at all the usual statistics about baseball teams, players and matches, going back over decades. Juggling with these in a huge database, they came to the conclusion that hardly any of the performance figures correlated closely with winning. All the defensive statistics about pitching and catching seemed to make no difference. The only two stats that were directly linked with winning matches were the on-base percentage I mentioned earlier and the slugging percentage, which is the number of times the team gains a base for each hitter that comes to the plate. All the rest of the normal averages and percentages were almost irrelevant.

So the A's started looking at more obscure statistics. They found data that tracked exactly what had happened to each individual ball put into play in major league baseball over a period of ten years. They looked at the story of each ball – the exact point on the field where it landed, how fast it travelled, whether the fielder stopped it cleanly, even whether the runner on second base chose not to hurry on to third because of a particular fielder's good throwing arm. All these events were given values, in terms of fractions of runs.

The stats were squeezing the idea of luck out of the game. That fielder who put the runner off from making an extra base was improving his team's position in the game by a small fraction of a run. If that happened often enough, it might make a loss into a win. But that had never shown up in baseball statistics before.

You can't eliminate chance and coincidence altogether. In all sports, things happen that shouldn't. Wrong decisions are made by officials, or pure luck intervenes. Players, managers, fans and journalists traditionally look at a bad decision that has caused a team to lose unjustly and mutter that the luck evens out over the course of a season.

It would be good if it did, but that would only be by coincidence. It is not impossible, in the competitive cauldron of the English Premier League, that football referees are minutely less likely to give a penalty against the home team on the hallowed turf of Manchester United's Old Trafford ground than at Fulham or Aston Villa. If that happened, what counterbalancing bias would necessarily make it even out?

But recording and analysing every component part of every play certainly changed the perspective at Oakland. It created an abstract value for each event, irrespective of whether, for example, a hit was caught or bounced just in front of the fielder.

Any ball hit anywhere on a baseball field had been hit just like that thousands of times before. The ten-year records showed that a hit to grid point #968, travelling at a certain speed and trajectory, was similar to 8,000 almost identical hits. Of those previous hits, 92 per cent went for a double (getting the batter safely as far as second base), 4 per cent went for a single and the other 4 per cent were caught by the fielder.

Under the new analytics system, based on all the past data, the hitter was credited with half a run and the pitcher was debited half a run. If the fielder happened to get to the ball and catch it, that fielder would be credited with saving his team half a run.

Instead of looking at the individual ball and the actual dramatic events on the field, the system was effectively treating that ball as the average of all similar balls. It was modelling at work. If there were 100 balls just like that in a season, there would be four catches and 92 doubles – and it didn't matter whether this particular ball was one of the catches or just adding to the doubles tally.

The game itself, its history over ten years, was telling the Oakland A's statisticians how valuable these events were, just as buying transactions send signals from the market. If you knew how valuable each event was (its 'expected run value'), you could calculate exactly what a player's contribution had been, over a game or a whole season.

Using this kind of information, Billy Beane and his colleagues could make smart, counterintuitive decisions about their priorities and their spending.

Resource allocation became largely a matter of fact and logic. Losing a big hitter who was also a brilliant fielder, Beane could decide that the cheap replacement who could match the hitting but was a sluggard when it came to fielding was still a good bet. The numbers showed that the weak fielder would cost the A's one run every ten games, but his hitting would more than make up for that.

The traditionalists scoffed, but the team won and kept on winning. The Oakland A's had an edge that let them substitute logic for money, and it stood them in good stead, until the other teams woke up and started copying these techniques.

I liked *Moneyball* as a film, and you can see why. It's an enjoyable movie. It didn't turn me into a baseball enthusiast, but it was certainly the best Hollywood film I'd ever seen that made statistics the hero. And as a parable for what needs to change in marketing, I thought it offered a lot of interesting and memorable lessons.

As I watched the scenes where the tobacco-chewing coaches and former players sat around the table and winced at Beane's explanations of how the new regime would work, I couldn't help thinking of meetings I had been in with confident, respected and vastly experienced marketing experts. Like the baseball coaches, they could see the world was changing and that that would mean their roles would have to change, too. They didn't like it, either. But when the team starts winning against the odds, it gets harder to fight what's going on.

Brandz Meanz Heinz

*An Institute of Practitioners in Advertising Effectiveness
Awards silver winner*

Do you believe in brands? Heinz does.

It's easy for anyone to believe in the power and accumulated equity of a great global brand when the world looks 'normal'. It's not so easy when the impact of recession and a world financial crisis has consumers across the country wondering whether their jobs and savings will survive and cutting back drastically on every kind of spending.

In the wake of 2008's economic collapse, research showed that more than half of all families had to cut down on their grocery shopping. People bought less, cut out luxuries and switched to cheaper brands. Supermarket private labels had never had it so good.

In the first quarter of 2009, Heinz was losing share to own label brands in all its core categories, including classic products such as Heinz Baked Beanz, Heinz Tomato Ketchup, soups and salad cream. A million housewives every day picked up a can of beans and said 'I wonder if we could manage with something a little bit cheaper.'

Heinz was on the way down, the own brands were on the up, and the unsentimental supermarkets were accentuating the trend by pushing through price increases on core Heinz products. With shoppers' buying decisions increasingly determined by price, Heinz was confronting a major test of its faith in the strength and value of its brand. Field studies showed that even diehard Heinz loyalists – normally unmoved by price differences or promotional activity – were being prised away from their commitment to the company.

But, faced with the options of lowering prices, scrapping it out in a promotions war with the cheaper products and the own labels or staking everything on the enduring virtues of its brand, Heinz took the bold step of sticking to its guns.

The campaign Heinz introduced in response to this ugly situation was simple and direct. If it had failed, it would certainly have been called arrogant and complacent. But it didn't. In the face of all the pressures, the new campaign reasserted the position of Heinz as cock of the walk, king of the heap, the unsubstitutable best in the clutch of categories where it had reigned for so long.

'It has to be Heinz' would only work if it won the assent of the consumer. If it provoked a reaction that said 'Oh no it doesn't – not at that price', it could even have backfired and accelerated the downward trend.

The marketers at Heinz gambled on people's emotional belief that Heinz was the only brand, for certain products, that could meet their needs at certain times. They sought to emphasise the brand values of comfort, feeling good and unique flavour, and the associations with childhood, love, security and family. Yet they knew that hard-pressed shoppers, at the point of purchase, would be weighing these emotional intangibles against the hard fact of a premium price.

The key insight was the recognition that even those who traded down to own label beans or ketchup did so with regret.

They felt they were losing something, in return for saving their money. And if shoppers were feeling that loss, then there was still something powerful that could be built on to persuade them that saving a few pennies simply wasn't worth it.

Bringing 'It has to be Heinz' to life in a major TV campaign involved identifying a posy of familiar real-life moments that generated smiles and recognition. The activities involved – chip-stealing, puddle-jumping, leaf-kicking and so on – were not exactly Olympic sports. But they were all strongly associated with positive values such as love, families, children, warmth and friendship.

Behind the heavyweight television launch, there was a low-key 'dripped' TV campaign aimed at maintaining recency and ensuring that shoppers were reminded of Heinz immediately before being presented with the lesser alternatives. Radio played a part, too, and Heinz worked hard to extend the campaign theme into the supermarkets to win more and better shelf space for its products.

The risks paid off, and the 'It has to be Heinz' campaign achieved what it set out to do. By honouring the Heinz brand equity and rebuilding loyalty, it had an immediate impact on sales volumes.

In the darkest days of early 2009, Heinz had been right

at the bottom of the list of the Top Ten food manufacturers, with sales slumping by 10 per cent over an 18-week period. One year later, it was the fastest-growing Top Ten brand, with 10.2 per cent growth. Year-on-year unit sales totals across Heinz were up by 6.9 per cent, and sales by value had risen 3.9 per cent.

The campaign was backed up by a certain amount of promotional activity, but much less than other FMCG rivals were using. Average unit prices were actually edged up (from 91p to 92p) and great care was taken, in the modelling work around this campaign, to avoid any misattribution of effects by separating out the impact of tactical promotions from the main strategic campaign.

The nominal category titles for the five much-loved Heinz products involved make most of them sound completely inedible. They are, officially, thick sauces, ambient salad dressing, beans and baked kids meals, and wet ambient soup. That's ketchup, salad cream, beans and hoops, and soup to you and me. These featured products all made market share gains of 4.5 per cent in the 18 weeks to 21 February 2010, largely at the expense of own label.

Unadvertised Heinz brands, outside these categories, showed a less impressive fightback. They continued to lose market share, but only by a tiny amount, effectively stemming the flight to cheaper own brand alternatives.

The most spectacular indication of the turn-round in the fortunes of the 144-year-old company was the 11 per cent growth, over 12 months, in both the volume and value of sales of the five core brands featured in the advertising. This compared with an equivalent fall of 8.5 per cent in the previous year.

Research from Nielsen showed a clear seesaw effect, with the 11 per cent boost for Heinz mirrored in an 11.5 per cent fall-off in supermarket own brand sales.

But people in the marketing discipline at Heinz have always been very keen to know what works, why and how much. The dangers of raindancing have long been recognised, which has made the company a long-term enthusiast for modelling and analytics. The modelling in this case was in the hands of Louise Cooke, one of London's most experienced business econometricians and a fellow judge, with me, for the analytics aspects of the IPA Effectiveness Awards.

Under Louise's guidance, four separate volume models (for beans, soup, ketchup and salad cream) were constructed, to allow Heinz to split out and examine the effects of 'It has to be Heinz'.

In order to isolate the contribution made by the campaign, the models took account of all other Heinz marketing (past and present), competitor activity and environmental factors that ranged from the weather to unemployment levels. Pricing, display and other elements of trade activity were also factored in.

The modelling highlighted the immediate and positive impact of the new campaign. In the short period from its launch in October 2009 to the third week in February 2010, it delivered an extra £12 million in UK sales revenue and an estimated £4.25 million profit. Total media spend was a modest £2.3 million, making the revenue return on investment (ROI) £5.29 for every £1 spent and the profit ROI £1.87.

Brand theory says that a huge global brand like Heinz

embodies generations of trust and emotional heritage that imbue it with a special value and a special place in its customers' lives. But the experience of Heinz, in the face of a brutal recession that directly affected its customers' food budgets and made the brand's values compete head-on with the lure of lower prices, proves that just having this accumulated brand equity does not guarantee safety. Sales sagged, despite the Heinz heritage.

Detailed modelling of the effects of the 'It has to be Heinz' campaign shows, beyond doubt, that this was the reason for the brand's abrupt recovery from its ominous nosedive. Further exploration of the models and their outputs will no doubt offer more insight into how to deal with future crises. But at least, for now, the marketers involved can be sure they did the right thing and that their actions, in placing brand values front and centre of a major TV campaign, had a direct causal connection with the company's ability to turn its fortunes around.

'Half the money I spend on advertising is wasted.
The trouble is, I don't know which half'
— John Wanamaker

CHAPTER 7

The Curves Show it: 80 per cent of Companies Underspend!

Four companies out of five stop spending too soon and miss out on extra sales and easy profits. How looking at the response curve and the profit curve can tell you whether to stick or twist.

We have already talked about analytics giving you a sense of what has worked and what hasn't – a backwards-looking view of which marketing levers you've been pulling and what effect each of them has had.

Marketing is a strange activity. Imagine you've got a black box, with a row of red lights on one side of the box and a row of switches or buttons on the other side. You press different buttons, and you see that different lights come on. The big conundrum, for marketers, is to try to understand just how the box is wired up. You press this button and this button and that one, in combination, and this red light comes on over here. And if you press a different combination of buttons, another light comes on.

Now what you would ideally like to be able to do is open up the black box and see for yourself how it is wired up inside. But that can't happen. So what you're actually having to do is try to figure out, by trial and error, how the thing works.

Modelling can help you work that out. As a marketer, you have pressed a lot of buttons, in various combinations, over the last couple of years.

You've probably been pushing buttons like crazy, but not necessarily in a systematic, scientific way. You've just been doing the stuff that marketers do – making things happen, juggling your budgets, getting behind products, spending more here and cutting back there.

But whatever model you and your colleagues have in your heads about how marketing and the market interact, you know it's necessarily pretty rough and ready. There are too many variables and their interaction is too inscrutable for anyone to hold it all in a single human brain, net out all the pros and cons and ups and downs and come up with anything approaching answers, rather than guesswork. There are simply too many data points for the mind to contemplate.

Computers, however, like lots of data points. The more the better. And you already have data that records all that marketing activity of yours and all the sales results that seemed to follow and may or may not have been the direct consequences of all those actions you took.

If you are not mining the huge amount of information that's there in your datasets, you are ignoring a vast set of clues to what has really been happening. It's like a detective who fails to realise that an enormous amount of evidence has been left behind, that the killer has left a trail of clues that can be analysed and interpreted.

But the evidence won't be in a nice, easy format that you can just read off. It'll be hidden in the data. It won't be neat, linear connections that say 'I pressed Button A and Light 2 came on.'

You are more likely to see results that say 'I pressed Buttons A and B together and Light 2 came on. But then when I pressed Buttons A and C, Lights 2 and 3 both came on.' And it will all be randomised up and presented in formats that are hard to untangle.

Looking at this stuff with the naked eye, you just wouldn't be able to discern the patterns. You need a mathematical technique that will unravel all this complexity for you. That's what modelling does. And the magic of it all is that it ends up effectively telling you how the black box is wired up.

The business value of this lies in its practical impact on your potential future performance. In future, if you want Lights 2 and 3 to come on, you know that you can achieve that by pressing Buttons A and C – newspaper advertising and in-store price promotions, for example – and not Buttons B and D, which might represent TV campaigns and local radio commercials.

In the real world, though, what modelling can tell you is more quantitative than we've been talking about up to this point. So it's not just 'Press Buttons A and C and Lights 2 and 3 will come on', but 'Press Button A for three seconds and Button C for five seconds and Lights 2 and 3 will come on for one minute.' And, even more significantly for campaign planning, the good news might be that 'If you press both buttons for six seconds, both lights will stay on for a minute and a half, giving you more impact for little extra effort.'

The fact is, there will usually be a dynamic, non-linear relationship between the amount of effort you put in and what you get back. The graph that shows this is known as a response curve. It allows us to look at the cause and effect relationship, as demonstrated by the factual evidence of the recent data.

For example, if we have the spend – on television, or print, say, or online advertising – on the horizontal axis and the outcome – usually sales, but it could be brand awareness, for example, or website visits – on the vertical axis, that will give us a curve. This curve will show us the cause and effect relationship in action. If I look at increasing spend on the horizontal axis, I can see immediately what effect that will have on the outcomes.

The response curve lies right at the heart of all our techniques for forecasting the future and optimising our performance. This is modelling at work.

The variable we pick for the horizontal axis is very often spend, but it could also be something like price, if we want to examine the effect of changing the price of a product on the revenues we'll get from it. Would dropping the price increase volume so dramatically that overall sales revenue would rise? Would edging the price up allow us to increase revenue with no appreciable loss of volume? In some markets, under some circumstances, it can be shown that increasing the price would mean bringing in extra revenue that would otherwise be left on the table.

Once we have a response curve that accurately reflects and matches the behaviour of products in our markets in the recent past, we have a tool that we can also use for forecasting.

Once we know what effect an extra tug on one of the marketing levers has had in the past, we can begin to make useful forecasts about what we should do to achieve the results we want in the future. How much do I have to turn the dial to do what I need to do? How much cash do I need to allocate to online advertising to lift sales to my target level? What would I have to spend to bring an extra 50,000 visitors to our website?

Response curves vary, fairly obviously, as shown in Fig 3. If adding to your spend added to your sales in a directly proportional way, on and on, for ever and ever, your response curve would be more of a response slope. It would be nothing more complicated than a straight, upward-sloping diagonal line.

But that's not what happens in the real world. You don't get a linear response curve like that. At some point, in the world of practical marketing campaigns, you start to see diminishing marginal returns.

This means that you have already thrown so much resource at the campaign that adding more spend gets you progressively less and less in the way of results. Where the response curve was previously climbing steeply, you are now into the area where, say, doubling your spend no longer doubles the sales. The curve rolls over the top, or at least, in the first instance, starts to flatten off, as shown in the upper curve here.

Fig 3. Diminishing returns and S-shaped response curves

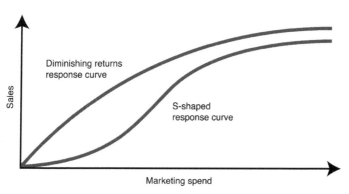

This diminishing returns curve is the classic centrepiece of the whole marketing returns analysis. But it doesn't always take the same rounded-off form. Indeed, its shape can be a good deal more exotic.

The response curve can be S-shaped, for example, starting almost flat or with a slow climb, then taking off and getting steeper and then, finally, flattening off again at the top, so that it forms a lazy, elongated S. The pattern this represents is the familiar one where it takes a certain critical mass of marketing investment to get a product's momentum going, so that some considerable spend is needed before it starts to break through and become visible. This is followed by the glory days, when the rate of climb is at its steepest and adding more spend generates higher and higher sales in a gratifyingly predictable way. And then, of course, comes the roll-off at the top of the curve, where saturation point is approaching and throwing more money at it simply doesn't shift enough extra product to justify the extra investment.

The perplexing question about S-shaped curves is why there has to be this threshold effect, the near-flat section at the front end where it seems resources have to be pumped in without any immediate return. Is it inevitable? Marketers would love to be able to target the right customers right from the off and get rid of this phase. Why can't we just get it right and get straight onto a steady upward curve?

When you look back over your historic dataset for the last two or three years and examine how you've spent your marketing money, it is highly likely that the data will reveal an S-shaped curve. This may be simply because you have deployed your resources inefficiently. But it may not be your fault. There may be factors entirely beyond your control that make this inevitable.

In a perfect world in which you could identify your ideal target audience for a UK consumer campaign and know that every one of these people watched a show like *Coronation Street*, you could focus your budget on that one opportunity and be certain that your television advertising would have an immediate effect.

The latest technology now allows such targeted advertising. If you are trying to buy access to television audiences, the new methods, using digital boxes in people's homes, make it possible to focus accurately and exclusively on the markets and demographics you need to reach.

In the old days, if you had unlimited funds, you could buy slots in the Super Bowl coverage, and that would reach almost everyone in America who watched television. But you can now also buy a media package that will enable you to target housewives aged 30 to 45 in Detroit. You can be that specific. It is expensive, but it can be done.

But if you don't do this, you have to buy a package that spreads your money across different parts of the country and different demographics, and some of that spend will inevitably be wasted, or at least diluted. There is an initial quantum of money that must be spent, however inefficiently, to ensure that, within the campaign, you are able to make your first contact with your target customers. You have to get beyond that level of investment before you start to really reach people and communicate effectively with them.

In this case you can't lop off the front end of the lazy S-shaped curve and cut straight to the chase, because of the way you have bought the media. But if you did target your media perfectly, you might escape from the S-shaped response curse.

But there are, of course, some marketing activities that can be targeted very precisely indeed. You can send a field sales force in to talk to exactly the people you need to reach, even ranking them in order of importance. You can segment direct mail audiences at a very granular level. You can use online techniques that allow you to follow up click-throughs and ensure that you are only ever talking to people who have shown by their actions that they are interested in what you have to offer.

Where these marketing approaches are appropriate for a particular industry and market, it should be possible to banish the S-shaped curve and ensure positive, scalable returns right from the launch of your campaign.

The big mistake that people make in thinking about response curves is to think of the horizontal axis as being about time.

They think of the shape, with the rising slope, rolling over and starting to plateau out at the top, and they say: 'Yeah. That's it. My sales curve does look like that.' But they are very often thinking of the most familiar graphs that pass across their desks day in and day out, the ones that show their sales figures, week by week or month by month. The response curve is something different.

The response curve gives you a different kind of information. For example, Fig 4 tells you that, in a given period of time, spending £1 million would get you £5 million in sales, while spending £2 million would get you £8 million and spending £3 million would get you £10 million. That's a very crude example, but it illustrates immediately that there is probably a case for spending £2 million, rather than £1 million, as the return is clearly higher.

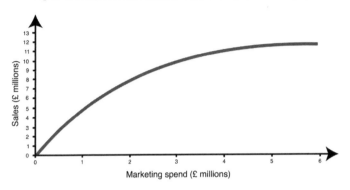

Fig 4. The response curve relates sales directly to marketing spend

The response curve is actually no more than a way of summing up a very large number of different what-if? scenarios. If I spend a million, what do I get? If I spend £2 million, how does it look? Should I even try to get the OK to spend £3 million?

These scenarios are always related to a specific time scale – in a week, a month or a year, what would I get back? But this is not a graph of the evolution of your sales over time.

There is no time axis for a response curve. Even in workshops, some people struggle to deal with this idea, so it is probably worth re-emphasising it.

But I have seen that, once people have got the basic idea of the response curve firmly in their heads, it has a remarkable impact on the way they think about business.

They become very curious about the relationship between their spend and their output and they want to explore what this means for their own products. This drags them, however unwillingly, in many cases, into taking an interest in modelling.

Later in the book I'll be talking about the Delphi process I often had to use in my international work with SmithKline

Beecham – effectively modelling without data, and surprisingly effective, if it's done right. But under normal European or American business circumstances, modelling, using as much relevant data as you can muster, is the way to put together a response curve. And while Delphi group meetings can throw up all kinds of useful insights, there is no doubt that working from the recorded facts of past performance produces better and more robust results.

Once you have a response curve, you can start to project forward and forecast, with some certainty, what will happen under various different sets of circumstances. Different scenarios can be combined, so that you can start to look at what would happen if you spent £1 million on TV and £500,000 on radio, while cutting the price of the product by 10 per cent at the same time.

Or you can focus on optimisation and making the most of your spend. You can get an algorithm to interrogate the response curves for you and tell you where the optimal points are on those curves.

So, for example, if you have a curve that shows money spent on the horizontal axis and sales value on the vertical axis, the tendency will be, as we've mentioned before, for sales to go up and up and up, as we plough in more money, and then eventually start to level off. At this point, though, let's assume that I still carry on spending more and more money. So if you plotted a cost line on the graph as well, this would carry on rising steadily with each extra pound that I spent on my marketing. And we would eventually get to a point, as the response curve continued to flatten out, where I was paying out more than I was getting back in extra sales. The lines would cross.

If you then plotted another line, a profit curve, you would see that it went up, reached a maximum and then started to turn down again, eventually moving right down and descending into negative territory.

Looking at these three curves together in Fig 5 below – the sales line, the marketing costs line and the profit line – makes it easy to see exactly what is going on.

Suddenly, it becomes quite straightforward to identify the optimal spend point, which is, after all, the elusive Holy Grail of marketing planning. The optimal spend point is simply the topmost point of the profit curve.

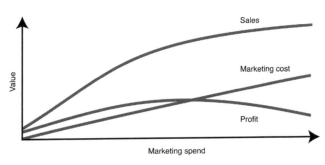

Fig 5. **How sales and profits respond to steadily increasing marketing spend**

All these response curves and associated profit curves apply to a specific period. As we said earlier, it is important to remember that these charts do not have an axis that represents the passage of time. Time is *not* something that is represented on a response curve. The response curve is a snapshot that illustrates the relationship between, say, marketing investment and sales value within a fixed period of time.

Generally speaking, the chosen period for which these curves are calculated will be short. It could be a month, or even a year, but in practice a one-week period is probably the one that's most frequently used.

In this case, the curve will be showing the marketer what the optimum spend per week should be. Once you know that, you can say 'Right, I want to spend £10 million over three months. How should I spend it?'

Rather than piling in with a £10 million spend in the first rush, or timidly spreading the £10 million out evenly over 13 weeks, you can work out how to optimise the impact and effectiveness of this spending over the period in question.

Spending the whole £10 million in the first week, for example, would certainly be a mistake. It would ensure that you were way up on the flattened top of the response curve and you would clearly be wasting your money.

You would probably find that only the first £1 million or £2 million was valid in the first week, because beyond that you would have saturated the market. However much more you spent at that point, you would hardly shift any more product. So the trick is to know, in advance, how far you should go and when you should stop and conserve your ammunition. You need to figure out what the optimum spend is for each week over a period of time – and then make sure you never spend more than that.

That is exactly what the optimisation algorithms within marketingQED's modelling software package do for you. They show you how your budget can be spent to achieve the targets you have identified.

So if, for example, you are a marketer who has been given a budget of £10 million to be spent over a period of three months, the optimisers will tell you how best to do that, optimising across all your different response curves and all your different marketing activities.

You may well be looking at a set of different response curves – a television curve, a radio curve, an online campaign curve and maybe some others, too – and moving money around between them to get the best possible effect. Fig 6 takes two of these curves (for radio and online) and illustrates why it is a good idea to move money around to get the optimal outcome.

What we can clearly see here is that taking money from radio, where the curve is getting flatter, and spending more on the online activity will increase overall sales. You gain more sales than you lose by making this switch. To be precise, we

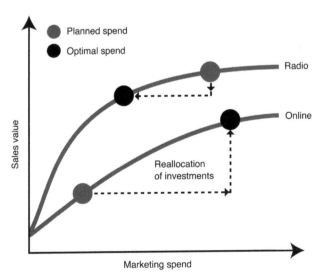

Fig 6. In this situation, optimisation calls for less radio and a lot more online

should really be looking at profit, rather than sales value, here, but I have deliberately chosen a simple example to illustrate the idea.

This is the whole basis of optimisation. The aim is to ensure that you spend your money where it generates the best return.

Alternatively, you may need to take the opposite approach and do a bit of reverse engineering. If there's a factory that needs to be running fully loaded to be efficient and that dictates a certain sales target for the next three months, the big question may be 'What am I going to have to spend over this period to make sure I hit my sales target?'

Effectively, you are looking at the same response curves. But instead of finding the appropriate budget figure on the *horizontal* axis and reading off, from the graph, what that will represent in sales, you can find the required sales figure on the *vertical* axis and read off what weekly spending figure that will imply. It won't be quite that simple, as there are momentum effects that cause sales to carry over to later weeks, based on what you spent earlier, but you get the general idea.

Knowing the optimal spend per week, along with the carryover effect, makes it relatively easy for an optimiser algorithm to roll the figures up and derive an annual budget that represents the optimal spend across the year. You can produce an overall annual profit response curve, which is often a very enlightening exercise.

Given an accurate annual response curve like this, it is obvious that some companies will find that they operate close to the optimal spending point.

But, believe me, two decades of business experience has shown me that such companies are definitely few and far between.

More – many, many more – will find themselves looking in horror at this curve and wondering how they could be so very far away from the optimally effective spending level.

And are they above, or below, the optimum point? Which side of the rounded top of the curve do they find themselves on? Are most companies overspending or underspending?

The underspenders are all in a position where, according to the evidence of the econometric models based on the recorded time series data of their past activities, they could increase their profits just by being willing to spend more.

The overspenders, however, are simply throwing money down the pan by spending on irrelevant and superfluous marketing activity that does nothing to add to their profits.

Neither implies particularly shrewd or scientific management performance. But which is the besetting sin we see most often?

The answer – as trailed in the title of this chapter – is that the vast majority of the bigger companies I have worked with, across many different sectors and industries, have regularly, consistently and dramatically UNDERSPENT.

The curve overleaf, in Fig 7, shows a typical situation. Spending more money, more effectively, gives you a double benefit. The first benefit is the gain that's achieved just by spending the original budget in a more effective way. The second comes from spending more money, again in an effective way.

When I say that 'the vast majority' of companies underspent, I am talking about something like 80 per cent.

That's right. Four companies out of every five that I have worked with have wasted the opportunity to increase their profits just by doing a bit more of what they were already doing and investing more in their marketing.

Fig 7. Falling short: the curve tells you how much to speculate to accumulate

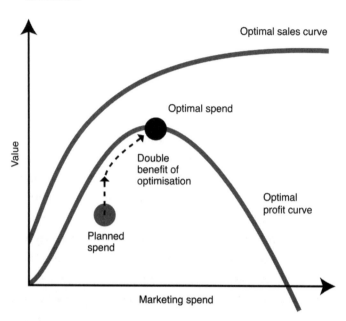

This is important information, and every analyst who has done this kind of work will immediately recognise it to be true.

Four companies out of five waste the opportunities they have created and leave profits on the table by spending less than the optimal amount on their marketing.

How many CMOs know this? Not many. Would they like to know? I think they would.

If they knew they were underspending, and by how much, these senior marketers would, for example, be equipped to go back to the company's board and present a reasoned business case that said: 'Give me £x million more to spend on this and I will get you a return of £y million.'

At the moment, that is a kind of conversation that rarely happens, as neither the precise amount needed nor the predicted return can be pinned down without proper modelling.

The word 'underspending' is pretty loaded, of course, and I need to make it clear that it is being used here in a fairly precise, technical sense.

What I mean when I talk about 'underspending' is that these companies are failing to maximise the opportunities open to them by stopping investing too early. On the profit curve diagram, they are to the left of the maximum, and therefore failing to optimise their activities.

There's a very good reason for this, and it's to do with the difference between marginal profit and average profit.

If you visualise a normal profit curve, like the charts above, it will go up in a parabola – like the stream of water from a hosepipe – starting to flatten out at the top of its arc, before falling away again. It's important to note again that this is not a curve of sales against time. There is no time element here. It is the curve that shows spending on one axis and the profit generated by that spending on the other. And what happens is that most companies find themselves to the left of the peak. They never get to the top of the profit curve.

Economic theory says that you should spend and keep on spending right up to the point where your profit is at its maximum. But, of course, people can't help noticing diminishing returns as they get towards the top of the arc. The benefits from each additional unit of spending start to reduce. For each extra pound they spend, they get less and less back, so it doesn't look like a good deal, compared with the money they were spending before, when they were on the steeper part of the curve.

But that marginal profit, smaller and smaller though it is as they approach the top of the curve, is still profit. If your job is to maximise your profit, those last profitable returns that you get before you hit the point where further spending brings no more profit are important. Leaving them on the table is a mistake, for several different reasons.

Let's see how this works with some actual numbers, as shown in the chart below.

Imagine you have used modelling to derive a graph of the profits generated by a company's marketing expenditure. Let's suppose the curve this produced showed a fairly typical shape, as in Fig 8. Spending £1 million on marketing would get you £10 million profit, spending £2 million would get you £15 million profit, spending £3 million would get you £18 million, spending £4 million topped it up to £20 million, £5 million gave profits that were still £20 million and £6 million only generated profits of £18 million.

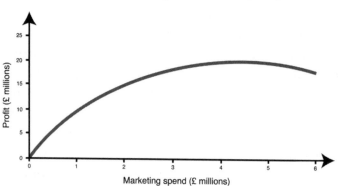

Fig 8. Altitude sickness: managers should watch profits, not ROI

In other words, the profit curve went up and up, started to flatten off, passed over a peak at the £20 million mark and then began to turn down again.

Faced with a curve like that, managers get mesmerised by the ROI on their marketing spend. They look at the dramatic 10 to 1 return they got on their first £1 million investment and they feel wonderful. When the spend rises to £2 million and they're only seeing a return of 7.5 to 1, they accept that the lowering of the average ROI is inevitable.

But when the next million, taking the spend up to £3 million, only brings in another £3 million profit and the overall average rate of return falls to 6 to 1, they tend to lose their nerve and put the brakes on.

In this example, that means missing out on the opportunity to raise profits from £18 million to £20 million, in a largely risk-free way, simply by investing another £1 million.

Logic says that marginal 2 to 1 return may not be glamorous, but it's worth taking.

Habit, however, says 'No, we'll stop there.' And companies, and managers, tend to be creatures of habit.

This is just an example, of course, and the use of nice, round numbers makes it easier to see what's going on. But the general assumption, across a large part of the world of business and finance, that a reduction in ROI is necessarily a sign that a company has taken a wrong turning is just laughable. In terms of business numeracy, it is on a par with the howler made by people who assume that if a company grows by 20 per cent one year and then shrinks by 20 per cent the next, it will end up back where it started.

In fact, by accepting that diminishing returns are inevitable but nevertheless carrying on spending to the top of the profit curve, a company will make the most of the opportunities presented to it.

And if that actually happens in more than about one case in five, I'll eat my hat.

But it's not just management's bad habits and sloppy thinking that come into play here. City analysts, the people charged with making judgments on behalf of investors about how well companies are doing, are equally mesmerised by what happens to average ROI.

These analysts will look at the money a company is spending on marketing and look at the company's sales and profits and do some very crude calculations based on comparing them.

Finance people will look at these numbers and say: 'Look, you're currently spending £3 million on marketing and you want backing to take that up to £4 million. But the rate of return, the average ROI, is going down. Why would I want to invest that extra million in marketing?'

We see this kind of thinking all the time, and it's fundamentally flawed.

Taking the average rate of return on investment as the way to evaluate how resources should be allocated across a firm is madness. It is simply not logical.

The difference between average and marginal return on investment is crucial. Anybody who's done economics will know this, as it's a fundamental part of economic theory. But even those who know it tend to lose sight of it – or perhaps they choose not to be the person who stands up and tells the boss that he's basing big decisions on false logic.

It sounds awful to say it, but the reason people calculate

average ROIs is simply, to put it crudely, because they are easy to calculate. But they are highly misleading, and you just cannot use them for decision making and resource allocation.

I once saw a statistician who really should have known better – from another consulting firm – presenting some results to a big pharmaceutical company. The mistake he had made was that he had calculated average return on investment figures for sales and marketing expenditure in a number of different countries and they had formed a key plank of his recommendations.

'For this particular product, the ROI figure in the UK is 3,' he declared. 'In France, it's 4. Therefore, our recommendation is that you should put more money into France.'

That's just wrong. For a start, if you think back to the example we were talking about earlier, it is clear that the higher average ROI figure for France does not mean that you are on a steep part of the curve and that spending more will get you more. It could easily be the case that you had saturated out at what happened to be an ROI of 4, whereas in the UK there might be plenty of extra value to be had by spending more. You just can't tell by simply looking at average ROI figures.

In fact, of course, the general rule is that the more money you put into marketing, the lower your average ROI figure will be. Unless you are in the type of situation where an S-shaped curve applies, it is inevitable that the first investment you make will always produce the highest average ROI. The average figure will then work its way downwards from there. But you, as a business, should not be worried about that.

What you should be worried about is the marginal return on investment. What you want to be clear about is whether you can make more profit by spending more. If you can, and the rate of return on that new, marginal slice of investment money makes sense, then you should go ahead and spend it – in exactly the same way as 80 per cent of companies don't.

The essential question is very simple: 'If I spend an extra pound, what will the return on that spending be?' It's the extra pound that matters, not the average pound.

It all depends on where you've got to on the response curve. Where the slope of the curve is steep, you can keep piling in money and you'll get a very good payback.

If I offer you a deal where you give me £1 million and I give you £2 million back, that's good business for you.

That's what was happening in our original example when the overall marketing spend went up from £3 million to £4 million, total profits rose from £18 million to £20 million and the average ROI rate (for what that figure is worth) fell from 6 to 5.

Obviously if funds are scarce in a firm, and generally they are, it is possible that spending that million on another project, such as a new supply chain process, may yield a greater marginal return. That would be a good reason for not investing that last million in marketing.

But we all know that isn't the real reason for marketing's underspending. The real reason is that nobody actually has the numbers that would lead to a rational decision.

There's another key point here. In this case, we are considering extra investment in a context we have now explored very carefully, analysed, modelled and understood. We know how it works, what the market drivers are and how today's situation relates back to all the detailed performance data we have accumulated over the previous several years. So if the model forecasts that investing £1 million will bring a return of an extra

£2 million in profits, that should be a pretty robust prediction.

Compare that with all the uncharted unknowns that can affect the potential payback from investing the same budget in a new factory or a sexy new product launch.

Factories can be held up or become impossible to operate efficiently because of a hundred different and unpredictable factors, from planning problems to trade union activity. New product development sets the pulse rating, but everyone has seen the statistics. Most new products fall by the wayside, and even those that succeed will bring with them the requirement for their own marketing investments.

I would never belittle the importance of new factories, new products, acquisitions and all the other investments businesses need to make to grow and be profitable. But very few of these investments are as likely to deliver genuinely predictable profits as extra spending on tried and tested marketing activity for an existing product that can be shown to still be on the upward slope of the response curve.

The advantage of econometrics, of analysis and modelling based on thousands of recorded purchases and data points, is that it does tell you how the market works. It may not tell you why it works that way. But if we go back to our original example of the mysterious black box with the switches and the lights and the hidden and inaccessible wiring inside, we now have a way of relating our activities and inputs to the outcomes that will follow.

Without the toolkit that analytics makes available, can you really make a reasoned decision to go ahead and make the investment of that extra million?

How could you possibly predict, with any real certainty, that upping the marketing spend from £3 million to £4 million was going to deliver an extra £2 million of profit? You wouldn't have a clue what the payback would be. You would be guessing, so the extra expenditure would necessarily be a gamble – a punt, rather than an investment.

Modelling allows the fine tuning of marketing decisions and resource allocation. It gives the marketer the equivalent of an electron microscope, a hugely powerful tool for objectively examining the structure and reality of the market environment.

If I show you a postcard and a sheet of A4 paper and ask you which is bigger, you can answer that immediately, instinctively and with complete certainty. But if I trim two or three millimetres off one sheet of A4 paper and hold this up in one hand and another unaltered sheet of A4 in the other, you will not be able to tell me which is which. Human beings are not good at judging very fine differences. Modelling can reveal fine differences and correlations that humans simply can't fathom.

If you're the marketing director and you have no real understanding of what will happen if you increase or decrease this or that activity, you are not properly equipped to go in front of your chief executive and your CFO and argue the case for an extra million to spend. You can't be specific and confident about the return, and that, of course, is why it so often happens that senior management errs on the side of caution and says: 'No thanks. We'll keep our powder dry and hold on to the money.'

You need modelling to give you the assurance that you are justified in committing to that extra spend. Without that support, you are gambling, and professional people don't like to be seen to be gambling. That is why, so often, companies end up underspending on their marketing.

The same kind of problem arises when times are hard and budgets are being cut back.

You may have been spending £3 million a year and you are suddenly told the board is planning to cut that back to £2 million. That should not be an emotional matter. It should be a rational decision, based on whether £3 million is actually the best and most profitable amount to be spending.

If it is, it makes no sense to chop the budget back just because other departments are suffering budget cuts. It creates no saving for the company if marketing spending is reduced by £1 million and that results in profits falling by £3 million, as in the example quoted earlier in this chapter. In fact, it is pure madness. There is a very human temptation to want everyone to share the pain, but it is one that should be resisted, with the help of the evidence provided by modelling.

At the very top of the profits curve we described earlier, raising spending from £4 million to £5 million resulted in exactly the same profit. You spent an extra £1 million and it covered its costs, but there was no extra profit. Why would you ever want to do that?

Well, normally, you wouldn't. But you might, if, for example, you were very concerned to recruit extra customers and build market share. And if you took it even further and carried on spending beyond the top of the curve, you would be simply buying market share, as the extra spending would mean your profits started to decline.

That might be part of a very aggressive strategy, in which your longer term interests were served by taking customers away from a key competitor. Or it might be a question of consciously investing in keeping a franchise alive until an important and potentially profitable new product comes along. I've seen that done. But at least the profit curve would be flagging up to you exactly what was going on and what price you were paying for the privilege of enrolling these extra customers.

For obvious reasons, the profit curve is one of the most popular outputs from the modelling toolkit. But other useful curves can be charted, using the same kind of approach. A price/demand curve, for example, can be produced, with price along the horizontal axis and volume sold on the vertical axis. This gives you a steep downward curve, with sales volumes understandably declining as price increases. It allows marketers and product managers to figure out what the optimal price for a product would be and plot the different levels of profit that can potentially be generated at different price points.

All these response curves have stories to tell. Once you see what shapes they take on, informed by the vast amounts of historic time series data that have generated them, you can tell a great deal about how you should act to achieve your business objectives.

But they can change remarkably quickly, as markets change and develop, new products are launched and fads and fashions come and go. So it is important to keep updating them as often as possible. If the data is analysed just once a year, nobody can truly hope to be up to date with the latest influences and movements in the marketplace.

Desktop analytics is a game-changer. It makes all this and more possible, easy and affordable. And it means, for instance, that you can readily produce response curves for individual campaigns and advertising executions.

I've seen clients compare individual executions on the basis of their effectiveness, as revealed by the response curves. Comparing individual campaigns can pose problems, simply because one creative execution may be more appealing than another. Optimists always want to base their future predictions on the results generated by the most successful creative work, but the most prudent approach is to take an average, rather than the standout execution that's attracted all the attention and won all the advertising awards. You can always hope, but you can't necessarily plan that your new creative execution will be as successful and powerful as the best you've ever had before.

There are plenty of subtleties and complications that can be examined in this sort of work. For instance, there's the whole question of carryover, or 'adstock' as the advertising professionals like to call it. This is to do with the after-effects of an advertising campaign. If I spend a million one week and then turn the tap off, there will still be a residual effect, for some time to come, from the big surge in that first week. It will tail off, and it is possible to model that rate of decay in order to decide exactly when the next slice of my budget should be spent to create the optimum effect.

If I want to optimise spending over, say, three months, I will need to take account of questions of carryover that would be very problematical to handle without the aid of a proper mathematical model and the computing power to crunch a lot of numbers. But it's all doable. It's just a set of equations you can solve, and this is the kind of thing that is now embedded in the desktop software to allow non-specialists in the marketing department to get to grips with these concepts and come up with the right answers.

How the Dome of Doom Turned into a Winner for O2

An Institute of Practitioners in Advertising Effectiveness
Awards gold winner

When the O2 mobile telecoms company agreed a sponsorship contract for the naming rights to London's Millennium Dome, a lot of commentators thought it was taking a big risk.

The Dome, a huge circular white marquee held up by twelve 100-metre steel support towers, on the Greenwich Peninsula in East London, had been one of the big embarrassments of the whole millennium project.

Sitting right next to the Thames, it had instantly become a major London landmark. But it had run way over budget and attracted half the planned number of visitors. Since the Millennium Exhibition closed, on 31 December 2000, the Dome had been seen as a white elephant and a political football – and one that cost £1 million a month to maintain, even when it was not being used.

Talking of football, in early 2005, O2 was coming towards the end of a £6-million-a-year shirt sponsorship contract with Arsenal Football Club. Though this arrangement had been well timed, covering a period of great success during which Arsenal played wonderful football and won both Premier League and FA Cup honours, it was not a unique form of marketing communication. There were 19 other Premier League shirt sponsors and sponsoring a big football club was arguably something of a me-too strategy, an example of the raindancing principle at work. It was the sort of thing major brands always did – almost out of habit – without really knowing what contribution it was making to business success. No serious attempt had ever been made to quantify how much tangible commercial value the sponsorship had delivered.

The Arsenal contract ended in 2006, but O2 wanted to achieve a lot more with its new sponsorship deal. It wanted to spend the same £6 million a year budget to rebrand the Dome as The O2, a major music and entertainment centre, and then to use the identification with music to reposition O2 itself in the public's perception.

This was a bold, deliberate strategic move, but the risks were all too obvious. The Millennium Dome was tainted with negative echoes and O2 itself had no traditional association with music, whereas Virgin Mobile, for example, did, because of Richard Branson's record label and music shops.

While sports sponsorship had done little more than link the O2 name with a successful Premier League club, O2's marketers believed the tie-up with the Dome could give them something unique that they could build on. They wanted to 'turn customers into fans', to change the customer's relationship with O2 from the functional to the emotional and to differentiate their brand in an increasingly commoditised market.

The risk was there all right – and the payback was by no means guaranteed. O2's chief executive, Matthew Key, had to take the idea to his board three times before he was given permission to go ahead. But by June 2007, the revamped venue was ready to open its doors, kicking off with a sell-out concert by Bon Jovi.

As word got around that it was a great place to play, the top acts queued up to strut their stuff. Prince booked, and sold out, a series of 23 concerts. Rock royalty gave The O2 their blessing, with Rolling Stone Keith Richards calling it 'the best indoor gig there is'.

Within months, The O2 was acquiring a reputation as a world-class venue. Every major concert was sold out in advance, and that presented O2 with a golden opportunity to make the most of its sponsorship. The unique ability to offer customers the benefit of priority ticket booking for sell-out shows meant there was a desirable and exclusive advantage to being with O2.

Perceptions of the brand improved by leaps and bounds, vindicating an interesting insight – initially no more than a hunch – that had attracted O2 marketers to this particular sponsorship deal in the first place.

For while it was obviously the company's customers who enjoyed the benefits of O2's loyalty and exclusivity initiatives, it soon became clear that ideas like the Priority Tickets initiative were having their most powerful impact among non-customers.

This effect – counter-intuitive though it seemed – was unmistakable. When the shift towards more positive attitudes to the brand was measured over the next few months and years, the improvement was always more marked among non-customers. And it was most marked of all among those non-customers who had experienced The O2 for themselves.

Experience of The O2 and awareness of the Priority Tickets scheme for O2 customers had a very significant effect on non-customers' willingness to consider switching to O2, which the marketers had identified as the single most important leading indicator for market share growth.

This was clearly a factor in the O2 brand's impressive progress over the next couple of years, during which O2 overtook Vodafone to become the market leader. But there were ten major O2 ad campaigns for new products and services during this period, and only two of these were focused on The O2, so it obviously wasn't the whole story.

Detailed modelling work was carried out to try to isolate and quantify the contribution made by The O2 sponsorship.

This showed that there was a strong link between awareness of The O2 and Priority Tickets, key brand metrics (such as awareness, consideration, bonding and 'voltage') and actual numbers of mobile connections.

The conclusion, according to O2's case study submission to the 2010 IPA Effectiveness Awards, was that The O2 sponsorship had been 'a key ingredient in the marketing mix, a major factor in differentiating the brand, and a cost-effective deliverer of business performance'.

One early sign of things to come was the positive correlation that was seen between Priority Tickets registrations and improved brand perception. This influenced the marketers to put more weight behind the trend with specific advertising campaigns in 2008 and 2009, with the result that more than 1 million customers signed up to Priority Tickets.

One key modelling exercise looked at the relationship between the advertising campaigns and gross connections (the number of new customers joining O2). This showed that the initial launch activity for The O2 had actually had little effect on new sign-ups, proving that the mere association with the venue – the badging of the Dome as The O2 – did not achieve any great impact. But a massive change occurred as soon as the Priority Tickets ads began. This is where the sponsorship started to pay off, as there obviously could not have been a Priority Tickets initiative without the sponsorship deal at The O2. By Q4 2009, Priority Tickets advertising could be shown to contribute 12 per cent of all new pre-pay connections and 11 per cent of all new pay monthly customers. And that meant big money.

In the mobile sector, churn is the marketer's nightmare. In the wake of the success of The O2 and Priority Tickets, churn was dramatically reduced. Customers who were aware of O2 Priority Tickets were found to be 10 per cent less likely to go elsewhere and 25 per cent more likely to recommend O2 to friends.

So there were clear paybacks, and it was important to use the modelling and other data to quantify just how effective the O2 initiative had been.

O2 invested a total of £44 million in The O2 sponsorship in 2007 to 2009, including payments for the naming rights, investment in the venue itself and marketing communications support.

The contribution to profit, based on incremental gross

connections up to December 2009, was £279 million, giving a notional ROI of 6.3 to 1. This was recognised as clearly understating the true return, though, as O2 declined to release the figures that would have enabled churn reduction to show up in the ROI.

Sponsorship often exists in a limbo of uncertain economics and questionable effectiveness. As the IPA points out, just 3 per cent of its effectiveness award submissions over the years have featured sponsorship, and not one, until the O2 campaign, has had sponsorship as its main ingredient.

Facts have been in short supply, and many sponsorship contracts are signed on a basis of gut feel and habit, making them classic examples of the raindancing syndrome.

Sponsorship is paid for with exactly the same sort of money that pays for TV campaigns or press ads, yet the lack of rigour behind the spending decisions is often breathtaking. Sponsors believe their brands have benefited from associations with sports teams, orchestras or events in the past, so they go on doing the same sort of thing in the future, without any real certainty of a causal connection between the activities and the presumed benefits.

By using disciplined econometric analysis and modelling to track and quantify the impact of its activity, O2 was able to prove that its sponsorship of what was once known as The Dome of Doom was succeeding. The company was able to refine and develop its tactics, isolate and examine the impact of this particular initiative and assess the ultimate contribution to profits. In a field where raindancing is still the norm, O2 chose to look the facts in the eye and bring mathematics and method to its marketing.

'Defer no time, delays have dangerous ends'
– William Shakespeare

CHAPTER 8

It's Time, too, as Well as Money

If data analytics and forecasts were in your hands straight away, within an hour or so, they could be helping with your day-to-day decisions. Desktop modelling is not just for big companies – or big strategy issues.

In my experience, different industries have different preferred media channels and often overspend on their favourite media vehicles. In pharmaceuticals, most companies will over-emphasise the sales force. In consumer goods, too much will usually be spent on TV advertising. Consumer electronics will favour print advertising and financial services will go for direct mail.

But timing, too, is an important factor in relation to marketing budgets. In consumer electronics, products move through the lifecycle so quickly that a new product that's launched this autumn will be old hat within a year.

In 2011, HP tried to break into tablet computers. But this market was a moving target, with obsolescence hovering at the factory gate. By the time HP's TouchPad tablet hit the shops, it was clear that it had missed the boat. The product was panned by critics, ignored by customers, savagely discounted by retailers and finally pulled by HP, 49 days after the US launch date.

That was exceptional. But flat screen TVs, for instance, were an example of a new product type that was tremendously popular when it first came out. Inside two years, however, everybody who cared had them. Others might buy later, in the normal course of events, when it was time to replace an old television, but the whole product category was essentially yesterday's news.

Within the TV manufacturing organisation, though, there will have been an individual marketing executive in charge of the budget and the advertising connected with the launch of the flat screen product. And two or three years later, this marketer is still likely to be holding a budget for this particular item. He will probably still be spending money, long after the product has passed through the usual lifecycle stages and reached the point where it is sitting on the mature side of the profit curve.

The result is that this money is being spent on a mature product that has exhausted its growth potential and offers no prospect of a profitable return on marketing investments. If there is any chance of making a return, it is likely to lie in a complete change of marketing tactics, spending less, but also spending it on, say, in-store promotions, instead of television. Unless, as sometimes happens, you can find some way of tweaking the mature product to give it a bit more life, a bit more zip, and thus reshaping the top of the curve and extending its effective life, it is usually time to take the money back and use it elsewhere.

At this stage, most, if not all, of the budget should normally be taken away from the mature product and shifted way back down the lifecycle to some newer product in the portfolio that is still growing and generating profits. A key part of portfolio management in industries like this is the art of managing resources across time. This is all about making sure that the business manages the development and lifecycle of its whole portfolio.

Given the brief, fleeting window of opportunity that's available for each new product in an industry like consumer electronics, timing is a key element. There is no time to go back and try again, if you find you have analysed the situation incorrectly and placed your marketing bets on the wrong horses.

This is exactly the kind of situation where modelling can help. Decisions have to be made fast, and they have to be right. But, traditionally, the modelling and forecasts that would directly support those decisions have been too slow to commission and too expensive to afford. Packaged software, sitting on an ordinary PC on the marketer's desk, provides the power to change this situation beyond all recognition. It allows dynamic portfolio management decisions to be taken in time to be effective, without relying on guesswork and limited personal experience, and without the need for marketers to cross their fingers, commit resources and hope for the best.

We've already mentioned, several times, the blunt fact that marketers are not very good at spotting, with the naked eye, where they should be placing their bets. They need a process and a support mechanism to help them do it more successfully. That mechanism has to be modelling. But in a fast-moving environment, the modelling must also be fast-moving. What the marketer really needs is to be able to read the dials in real time.

Imagine flying a plane by instruments, at night or in cloud. You are able to do it safely and effectively because your artificial horizon, your airspeed indicator and your altimeters are giving you instant feedback whenever changes occur. Now imagine trying to make that same flight if your instruments gave you the same measurements, with perfect accuracy, but with a one-hour delay. You couldn't do it. The measurements are important, but the fact that they are fed to you in time for you to act in response to changing circumstances is absolutely critical.

Most modern consumer industries – electronics, retailing and telecommunications, for example – are moving so fast that speed is of the essence. You may not need to change tack every few minutes or make constant course corrections. But you do need to be able to check in and see what's happening. You need some kind of early warning system that will tell you what's going on and what's going wrong, and you need to be able to see up-to-date real-time information.

It's not just a nice-to-have. It's an imperative. Because if you are still spending money on something – like flat screen televisions – that is not responding well to TV advertising any more, you are wasting that money. Maybe you need to switch your spending to in-store offers, to incentives for the retailers or consumer promotions that offer the flat screen TV buyer £50 off a DVD player. And if the market is sending you the signal that it's time to make this change, you need to be able to pick it up and act on it quickly.

In practice, when we talk about real-time information in this context, we mean that you are able to get a read on what's been happening in the last month or three months.

That may well contrast with your day-to-day assumptions about what's been going on – and if that's the case, the sooner you know about it and can start delving into the whys and wherefores, the better for the business. Data will be collected and correlated over a period of time, but what we are talking about here is the ability to get your analysis and your answers immediately – within a day, rather than two or three months –

whenever you get a new tranche of data to work with.

This is a lot faster than people are normally used to. American corporations are tuned to quarterly reporting these days, but that is usually a matter of reporting a limited set of figures, based around sales and profits. Marketing budgets are still almost always set for a full year at a time, though we all know that poor profit performance during the course of the year can often lead to the budget for the last quarter being slashed back.

Marketers' Q4 budgets are routinely raided and pillaged, simply because no-one has a sufficiently strong, clear and factual argument to defeat a chief executive or CFO who says 'We need to cut back on all our discretionary spending, and your spending will have to wait for the start the new financial year.' Marketing budgets look big and inviting. They seem easy targets for cuts. And they are duly raided.

Worse than this, though, is the cycle these bad habits set up. Marketers tend to be shrewd, ingenious people. If they know there is a likelihood the Q4 budget will be cut, they will often take evasive action by bringing their spending forward into the earlier parts of the year, so there is nothing left to be grabbed back later. Marketing spending then tends to be artificially frontloaded into the first half of the year, with marketers and financial management taking their eyes off the ball to play a cat and mouse game that inevitably distorts the timing of marketing activity and guarantees sub-optimal results.

By enabling marketers to prove, objectively, and quantify the value their activity is adding, analytics helps resist this knee-jerk tendency to cut marketing budgets as soon as something starts to go wrong anywhere in the business.

When the CEO comes along and asks questions like 'Why

do we have a marketing department, anyway?' and 'Why should I spend my company's money on marketing activity?', the marketing director or CMO needs to be ready with some convincing answers.

The only good answer to these fundamental questions is that marketing adds value, if it is done properly, by making a crucial and profitable connection between the product and the consumer. The business stands to lose if, for example, activity that should have taken place in Q4 is deferred to the following year. It is something of a novelty for the marketer to be able to show this, to quantify the value that may be jeopardised and to bring this element of objectivity to the party, through the use of modelling.

Realistically, of course, up to now, only big company brands in big markets have had the benefit of marketing modelling. What's more, this modelling has usually only been available, at best, once or twice a year, because of the cost and the lead times involved.

Those big brands in big markets that have access to modelling are just the tip of the iceberg. All the rest of the world's marketers have to manage without. And this means that something like 90 per cent of brands are flying blind.

Many of these blindfold marketers may be working with quite substantial regional products – a brand of biscuits in Poland, for example, may be a household name in its home market, even if it is unknown beyond the country's borders. But a brand like that won't be spending a huge amount on advertising, so it wouldn't justify investing £100,000 or £200,000, or whatever it might cost, to call in the specialists and get detailed analytics and modelling done.

I've seen figures that estimate that just 8 per cent of national brands in the UK spend more than £20 million a year on advertising. One brand in three has a spend of between £1 million and £2 million. But you're unlikely to pay £100,000 – 10 per cent of your budget – to optimise the spending on a brand with a total budget of £1 million or so. Most people would sooner take a chance and keep the money in working spend.

So the 90 per cent or so of the marketing iceberg that is below the waterline is not being analysed at all. The decisions are being taken on gut feel and intuition. People are placing their bets, not like the cool, professional gamblers who study the horses' form, watch the odds and only ever bet when all the factors are in their favour, but like the happy-go-lucky British punters who stick a hopeful tenner on an outsider they've never heard of on Grand National day.

It's no wonder there are fallers. Intuition isn't good enough. It's intrinsically flawed, and subject to every kind of bias. Experience is never sufficient, because the data sample size is inevitably going to be too small. Indeed, trusting to experience is particularly dangerous, because of the tendency to believe, whenever you get lucky, that it was because you got the analysis right and hence that you can trust your guesswork again next time round. That's how progressively bigger mistakes get made.

The opportunity my company is addressing – the potential for bringing usable, affordable analytics to the vast bulk of the iceberg that lies beneath the waterline – is revolutionary, exciting, transformational. It democratises analytics the way PowerPoint democratised the ability to make slide presentations. (I know that particular example cuts both ways, but big gains always bring some pain, as well.)

Instead of being excluded from the use of analytics and modelling by crude cost/benefit factors, companies will be able to decide for themselves whether to use the new tools or just keep on guessing. Within a few years, a decade at most, the tiny minority of companies with the unfair advantage of access to these facilities could turn into an overall majority.

I've spent a lot of time thinking about this, as you'd expect. And I've realised that one of the less obvious impacts of putting powerful analytics and modelling software on the PCs on non-specialists' desks is a change in the type of decision that these kinds of technology can be applied to.

Until now, analytics has only really been used to address big, strategic and essentially slow-moving issues. While we have developed models based on past data and used them to produce forecasts, there has always been a backward-looking cast to them.

It has been possible to draw up penetrating, insightful end-of-term reports or, perhaps, dip in and take the pulse of the brand every six months, or even every quarter. But, even leaving aside all questions of cost, the whole process has been far too slow to be used for tactical everyday decision-making.

There has been no effective way to tap its power and its insights to inform the cut and thrust of day-to-day business.

It's one thing being able to look back several months later and assess whether the decision to pounce on a particular one-off media-buying opportunity was a good one or not. It's quite another to be able to use the technology of desktop modelling to tell you, on the spot, on a particular day, whether to buy there and then or to hold on to your budget for another time.

One specific example of the difference this makes occurred when one of our manufacturing clients had the opportunity, on a Thursday afternoon, to increase the price of a key product in a major retail chain. If the change was going to happen, it needed to be implemented the next week, and the retailer needed to know almost immediately, by the next day. The sales team came to the insight team looking for guidance on whether the opportunity should be taken up or declined.

Using the desktop modelling tools, the insight team was able to crunch the numbers and come back with clear, unambiguous advice to go ahead with the price increase. The analysis suggested the net result would be positive and yield extra profit for the manufacturer that would otherwise not have been captured.

In the event, it was a very clear illustration of the potential of this new kind of tactical analytics. That agility and responsiveness had never been available before – to anyone, even including the biggest corporations.

Even where the cost of using analytics would not have been an issue, there would simply have been no possibility of getting an answer fast enough to be useful. And in this case, the manufacturer made a cool €4 million in additional profits from being able to exploit that specific opportunity.

Other companies will obviously find themselves in all kinds of situations where different but comparable marketing dilemmas crop up and short-term opportunities arise. But most of these questions have traditionally formed the bulk of the iceberg – the 90 per cent or so of all marketing decisions that are below the waterline and taken on the basis of gut feel, because using analytics has demanded time, as well as money.

The big change is that many of these issues are now becoming addressable through modelling for the first time. The sheer number of decisions that can now be based on sound factual data is massively increased, once desktop modelling can be made available.

The significance of this new decision toolkit is vast. Mistakes can be avoided and opportunities that might have seemed too risky to take on can be embraced.

Human beings are notoriously poor at estimating the true risks attached to situations where many different factors are involved.

We mix up fact and emotion. We make causal connections that seem to explain our successes, when careful analysis often shows that these connections are completely illusory. We tend to play safe too often. Worse than that, if we do decide that boldness is needed, we often pick the wrong occasions to be bold. So we frequently make errors in both directions, both causing losses and failing to generate profits when we could have done.

Even a minor improvement in day-to-day decision-making outcomes, repeated time and time again across a full year, can transform the performance – and specifically the profitability – of a company. If overheads and input costs are generally fairly constant, raising the hit rate associated with marketing decisions is one of the most direct ways of boosting profits. Bringing desktop modelling to bear on the multitude of smaller, tactical decisions, as well as the occasional big, strategic ones, is a powerful force for change.

We need to get away from the entrenched idea that analytics and modelling can only be exploited by rocket scientists.

People have been led to believe that this is such a specialist area that they can't hope to get their hands on it or their heads round it. They haven't been able to do it themselves, so they have had to hire specialists. Inevitably, a mystique grew up around modelling, accompanied by a belief that it was too complex for mere mortals. It was a closed world, and no-one with the necessary inside knowledge had taken it upon themselves to bust it wide open and make useful, practical tools available to ordinary people in ordinary businesses.

That's the challenge we have set ourselves – to make products that sit on PCs and can be driven by the people in the marketing department.

We've also addressed another significant shortfall in the delivery of modelling services, the overcomplicated outputs that were frequently incomprehensible to the analysts' audience in the marketing community.

Marketers would struggle to understand what the modellers were telling them, while the modellers – usually with no marketing experience themselves – would think their job was done when they had spewed out a barrage of numbers and equations and statistics. Statisticians know about statistics. What was so obvious to them it didn't need mentioning would often be completely obscure to the marketers.

As a statistician, I will look at a chart and be able to 'read' it, as quickly and easily as a violinist reading the dots or a layman reading a book. I can draw out, almost at a glance, the main messages and implications. But it's easy for us to forget that marketers – often bright people but with an educational background that is usually not based on developing quantitative skills – are unlikely to have that knack. They know their business, but they don't know mine.

So it is hard to look through the eyes of a statistician and see your graphs the way a marketer would see them. I'll be looking at a chart and adding things up in my head, playing around with the numbers. It's second nature to me. Marketing people are unlikely to have that easy familiarity with graphs and numbers, and it takes a real skill to talk about these things to marketers in terms that are understandable and mean something in the business context.

To tell the truth, I've seen some very confusing presentations by experienced consultants in this field. I've seen them present numbers in a format that is quite incomprehensible to anyone without a mathematical or statistical background, and then walk away, thinking their job is done.

It's not as rare as you might think. Modellers present marketers with tables of, say, price elasticities, without spelling out the significance of what they are showing. But elasticities are quite abstract numbers. They need simple, demystifying explanations.

Statisticians should not be afraid of saying 'Look, this price elasticity of minus 3 here means that if we increase our price by 1 per cent, we will lose approximately 3 per cent of our volume.'

That doesn't cheapen or dilute the value of their work. In fact, it makes the work more valuable, as it enables the marketers in the room to move quickly on to discussing how that would play out in the actual business.

The econometricians may quote a TV advertising elasticity of 0.1, which means that increasing the TV spend by 1 per cent will lead to a volume gain of 0.1 per cent. That doesn't sound like a recipe for success, but, of course, that's going to depend on the absolute figures involved. If the current TV spend is minimal and your FMCG item is already selling in huge volumes, it might be exactly what the marketer wants and needs to hear.

The worst presenters will even flash up a slide showing the

modelling equation they've used, without realising that everyone else in the room has just glazed over and given up trying to follow what's going on. If there's no real understanding of what the numbers mean and how they have been put together, the marketer is left thinking 'What do I do with that information? How can I use that?'

In the real world, people attending a presentation will listen and nod and hope they've understood what they have been told. But even those who haven't understood don't always say so, for all the obvious reasons.

As a result of all this, a high proportion of the material generated by analytics and modelling exercises gets taken back to the office, stuck on a shelf and never used, making it a complete and utter waste of money. The analysis bounces off the organisation and ricochets off into the void, when it could be going a long way towards guaranteeing better value from every pound of marketing spend.

If there's no traction, there's no value.

So the big, fundamental question is this. How do you make modelling available, understandable, usable, timely and inexpensive?

We are not talking about nice-to-haves here. The fact is, you can't do the job of the modern marketer properly without access to these tools. I know 90 per cent of all marketers currently have to try, but they are demonstrably shooting in the dark.

Because the high road of analytics-backed marketing has been too difficult, we have seen marketers stuck on the low road, relying on gut feel, intuition, instinct and experience. And it could be so much better.

There may be room for argument about that proposition

now. But as soon as one serious competitor in any market segment starts to benefit fully from using the new tools, it will immediately become imperative for that company's rivals to equip themselves with the same business weaponry, or risk being outgunned.

The pioneers who are the first in their fields to adopt desktop analytics, integrating modelling power with their own knowledge of the industry and the marketing context, will dramatically increase the efficiency and effectiveness of their marketing. With less waste and better decision-making, it will be like having a bigger marketing budget – and their competitors will soon feel the impact of that.

Sainsbury's and the £550m Idea

By 2004, Sainsbury's was going backwards. It had just been overtaken by Asda and like-for-like sales were in decline. So when a new chief executive, Justin King, arrived, his first priority was to turn the supermarket around.

King came in with guns blazing, launching an immediate attack on two very obvious weaknesses – empty shelves and uncompetitive pricing. He cut 6,000 prices, took on 3,000 new staff, made sure stock was there when shoppers wanted it and was rewarded with the first signs of like-for-like sales growth.

But something more was required. Sainsbury's management calculated that the company needed to increase sales by £2.5 billion in the next three years. And that monumental figure was simply too large for anyone to get to grips with.

It needed to be broken down – and it was, in a wonderfully clear calculation that hinted at how it could be achieved. Sainsbury's had 14 million shoppers every week. If each of them could be persuaded to spend £1.14 more a week, the job would be done.

The sum was simple: £1.14 x 52 weeks x 3 years x 14m customers = £2.5bn (all but the loose change). The mammoth task of generating £2.5 billion in incremental sales revenue was cut down to size when it was clear that it translated into getting every customer to spend just a little bit more.

Justin King himself had said straight away that he believed the recovery would be driven by getting existing shoppers to spend more, rather than by kidnapping competitors' customers.

The problem – and the opportunity – was that existing shoppers had fallen into routine, unadventurous shopping patterns, and Sainsbury's had not done anything much to shake them out of them. Research showed that this sleep-shopping habit meant customers were buying the same basket of goods, week in and week out, with little variation and no inspiration. If Sainsbury's could get people more interested and excited about their food shopping, and thinking about what they were buying, rather than just the prices, there would clearly be scope for capturing all those extra £1.14s that would add up to £2.5 billion.

The stimulus for this transformation was a simple idea, summed up in the phrase 'Try something new today'.

Customers would be nudged and tempted into breaking out of the rut. But almost before that could happen, it was vital that Sainsbury's own staff (or 'colleagues', as the company insists on calling them) changed their own behaviour and started trying new things themselves. The colleagues were given extra training and encouragement to talk to customers about new ideas, managers were urged to find new local suppliers and better ways of working and there was a general shift in the ethos of the business, in the direction of innovation and even risk-taking. 'Earning the £1.14' became a company catchphrase, as all 150,000 staff became involved in the initiative.

For the customers, there were new television campaigns and Tip Cards in the stores suggesting new recipes and novel twists on old ones. The slogan 'Try something new today' was everywhere. But the level of advice was deliberately down-to-earth.

'Try nutmeg on your spag bol,' shoppers were urged, and nutmeg sales quadrupled in weeks. 'Try roasting carrots with thyme' and 'Try frying sausages with apple slices and sage' the Tip Cards said, or even, 'Try hot cross buns in bread and butter pudding'. The simple, sometimes surprising, usually inexpensive, ideas to spice up and enliven everyday dishes caught the imagination and prompted at least 8 million of those 14 million Sainsbury's customers to try them out.

Over 200 million Tip Cards were given out in the stores, covering 325 separate ideas. Television commercials developed the same themes, running alongside campaigns featuring Sainsbury's long-standing relationship with TV chef Jamie Oliver. As total market spend in the supermarket sector grew sharply, Sainsbury's was able to ease back on its advertising, spending a little less in absolute terms and reducing its share of spend from 23 per cent to 19 per cent.

Far from suffering, the brand continued to score consistently high on measures such as customers agreeing with the proposition 'Sainsbury's is always coming up with new ideas', while brand image measures related to 'fair prices' and 'great products' climbed steadily.

Even more to the point, existing shoppers spent more, lost customers returned and 'Try something new today' proved a very helpful fit for store refurbishments and new store openings.

Sales grew, and continued growing for ten consecutive quarters, while the original target of £2.5 billion in extra sales over a three-year period was achieved three months ahead of schedule.

Down at the shopfloor level, sales of the products mentioned on the television and the point of sale Tip Cards went through the roof. Mangoes soared by 400 per cent. Parsnips rocketed, up 275 per cent. Sales of sausages, apples and pears all doubled. Even feta cheese sold 50 per cent more. Almost every single tip improved sales dramatically for the products mentioned.

Ingredients highlighted in the television campaigns naturally experienced the biggest growth in sales. Nevertheless, in the first month of a new Tip Card and point of sale display focusing on burgers, but unsupported by any other advertising, sales of lean steak mince kicked up by 74 per cent and burger buns sold 55 per cent more.

The remarkable effectiveness of the Try idea – even apart from its execution in television commercials – was something Sainsbury's was very keen to track. Since the early 1990s, the company had been one of the UK leaders in the use of econometrics and modelling to examine and isolate the effects and returns generated by its advertising and marketing activity.

According to Sainsbury's modelling data, the 'conventional' end of the Try initiative – the TV advertising – delivered a sales contribution of £1.35 billion over a period of 30 months. Based on a media spend of £55 million, that represented an ROI on the TV campaign of £24.55 per £1 spent, and a profit (using industry standard estimates, as Sainsbury will not release the actual figures) of just over £6 per £1 spent.

But that was the easy bit. What Sainsbury's management – and everyone else who had seen what was going on – wanted to know was what contribution had 'Try something new today' made, *apart from* its role in the television campaigns.

There clearly was something substantial and potentially quantifiable here, but isolating it would not be easy.

For the modelling team involved, one of the key issues was establishing what had *not* caused the uplift in sales at Sainsbury's. The marketing mix modelling that was developed specifically examined a wide range of factors in order to exclude them as explanations for either the sales contribution attributed to the TV campaign or the 'idea effect' of 'Try something new today'.

These factors that were ruled out included:
1.   stock availability
2.   pricing vs competitors
3.   Sainsbury's media spend
4.   competitors' media spend
5.   direct marketing and door-drops
6.   coupons at till
7.   weather
8.   special events (eg World Cup)
9.   Active Kids voucher collection scheme
10. Comic/Sport Relief sponsorship

11. new stores, extensions and refurbishments
12. competitor openings and closures
13. payday

The aim here was to try to isolate the specific value delivered by the idea itself, as distinct from the value delivered by the communications that carried that idea.

And the modellers' answer – £550 million in sales over two years – was enough to catch anybody's attention. According to the modelling reports, the impact of the 'Try something new today' idea manifested itself as 'a step-change in base level sales' that could only be attributed to the idea's implementation.

The award-winning submission to the IPA Effectiveness judges said that accelerated revenue growth had been generated for the supermarket as a whole, irrespective of the effects achieved through advertising activity. This was 'not simply a campaign effect by another name ' and was 'quite distinct from the enhanced sales effects of the Try TV advertising'.

The submission claimed the idea had led to a broad change in behaviour, unrelated to media spend, which had had a massive impact on sales, adding £137.5 million in extra profits to the bottom line over two years.

There's probably room for a technical argument about how precisely the effects of the idea can be isolated, and therefore what the final figures should be. But there is no doubt that the idea of suggesting, explicitly, to both staff and customers, that they should 'Try something new today' was both powerful and profitable.

The modelling was certainly able to provide a

mechanism for quantifying the effect, allowing a unique insight into the tricky question of how ideas can be valued. There was no need for the usual impressionistic story telling and myth-building on this occasion. Even if there was room for argument about the exact figures, there could be no argument about the fact that the modelling showed a substantial positive return on investment, above and beyond what was attributable to the conventional media campaign.

In the end, Justin King got the extra £2.5 billion in three years that he had called for. In fact, by the time the third year was up, Sainsbury's had overshot and hit the £2.7 billion mark. That is pretty convincing evidence that something unusual had taken place. King asked for a revolution, and that's what Sainsbury's willingness to try a new approach made possible.

'There are naïve questions, tedious questions,
ill-phrased questions, questions put after inadequate self-criticism.
But every question is a cry to understand the world. There is no
such thing as a dumb question'
— *Carl Sagan*

CHAPTER 9

Talking with Martians

Two intelligent beings from the red planet ask some of the awkward questions about modelling and forecasting. Do you need a hypothesis? How much data? How many variables? Where do events like tsunamis and 9/11 fit in? And how do you tell what's cause and what's coincidence?

Martian 1: You're using huge amounts of data to do modelling from which you can potentially create forecasts and predictions. Do you need to have a model in mind, a hypothesis for what you are modelling? Or is it more to do with this idea of 'boiling the ocean' – gathering in all this data, shaking it about and then just seeing what emerges?

GG: That's quite a difficult question, because there are different schools of thought on this. The distinction is really between a hypothesist approach and a context-free empiricist approach.

With the hypothesis approach, you are going to be influenced by what you believe you have learned from your past experience. Faced with the need to estimate the demand for a product, you'll say 'Right, I believe the demand for this is going to be driven by the price, the distribution it enjoys, the things we do in the way of promotions and advertising activity – and that competitors' pricing will also affect it.'

Now, the data set you have to work with will simply be the record of many, many past events – if you like, thousands of mini-experiments that have happened, week in, week out, over maybe a couple of years. What you are hoping to do is disentangle what has happened in each of those little mini-experiments. Because, like it or not, every change in the product and its environment – and, in particular, everything you did – will have had some kind of impact. It may have had almost no visible effect, or it may have a strong positive or negative impact.

You hope that the things that you've done, that were under your control, will have had a positive impact. But, to be honest, you may not have been operating to a coherent, all-encompassing master plan. You may have just thrown things together fairly blindly, doing what you could when you could and taking opportunities when they arose. Budgets, departmental politics, product or upgrade delays – there are all sorts of real-life reasons why people's plans get knocked out of shape. But all of this, everything that's happened, wanted or unwanted, is now lurking there somewhere, hidden in the data. And what you want is to be able to reconstruct what really happened.

It's like the problem the palaeontologists have when they go fossil-hunting and find a bunch of bones buried in the rocks. What happened, perhaps, was that millions of years ago, two dinosaurs met in some titanic struggle on the edge of a swamp somewhere, fought and mortally wounded each other and dropped down dead in a heap. When the bones are eventually uncovered, there may be no easy way of telling, at first, which bones are from which creature and what story they are telling.

The challenge is to unpick the puzzle and understand what has happened. And that same process of sifting through and decoding the message in the data is what we're trying to do. We're trying to see the impact of each of these individual factors.

So we can do it by saying 'Right, I believe sales is a function of all these factors. Now let's test this hypothesis against the data we have.' And when we do that, the data will effectively come back and say 'No.' Or maybe it seems to be saying 'Yes, here and here, but not here.' So parts of your hypothesis are tested and you're then refining it iteratively, as you go along, in the light of what the data is telling you.

That's one methodology, and it's the one most people would follow. It's the standard, econometrics, regression modelling, whatever people choose to call it.

The other way is the undirected, context-free empirical approach. Some people don't trust the idea of testing and refining a hypothesis because, as they say, you're immediately introducing bias and preconceptions.

They prefer the kind of modelling technique where you just throw all the data in, use the almost unlimited computing power available today and get the software to look for patterns, with no prior assumptions at all about what might cause those patterns or what they might mean. These systems often use neural networks or other data mining techniques and they are, literally, blind. They start from scratch, find correlations and draw your attention to them.

As it's become easier and cheaper and quicker to crunch enormous volumes of numbers, there's been more attention paid to this kind of thing. But few people try to apply this approach to solving practical business problems.

The problem is that although the number of potentially interesting correlations is vast, no-one would believe that a correlation was indicative of a causal relationship if it didn't fit a preconceived idea of what seemed sensible.

So all you are doing, with this approach, is applying the preconceptions after the correlations have been made, rather than before. There is also the question of which data to throw into the mix. The choice of that data set necessarily introduces the sort of bias the empiricist was so eager to avoid. You can't analyse everything, so you have to make a choice. And that choice involves imposing some sort of bias.

Martian 1: But you believe you can give marketers the best of both worlds?

GG: Yes. One of the reasons people get so excited about what we've developed for marketingQED is that we have blended both approaches to some extent.

We allow users to input a wide array of different data that they think may have an influence on a particular metric, such as sales. The software then searches for many different models, using different data series, perhaps, that fit the series being modelled, and that make sense.

This approach delivers a range of models that conform to what we might expect using a hypothesis approach. But we are not tightly limiting the hypothesis. For example, we might think a model that shows TV advertising had a large and positive effect on sales had the same degree of plausibility as one that showed an effect for online and print but no TV effect at all. As long as both had a positive effect, rather than a negative one, we would consider both as possible models. The hypothesis is constructed to cast the net widely in the hunt for good models.

All this can be done in a matter of minutes, as often as necessary. That means that marketers can take snap decisions – say, about whether to take up the offer of a cut-price media deal for a new campaign – almost as quickly as they could toss a coin, and with a far greater chance of getting the right answer.

Martian 2: That's very interesting. So do you have to know what you're looking at? When you get the results in front of you, do you have to know what they mean?

GG: Yes. I think you do. And I firmly believe now, having seen our software in action, that context makes a huge difference.

Everything is contextual. When you see a bump in the road, a twitch in the data, you need to be able to say 'Oh yes. I know what that was. I can account for this.' Then you can use various techniques to take it out – what we call 'dummying it out' of the data. So your background understanding of the context helps you account for it and recognise that it is not some spurious data point. You can't model in a vacuum.

Martian 2: Are there parallels between this sort of stuff and what they do with complex financial derivatives? And does that mean it carries the same dangers – the risk that things could go wrong because you can't see inside and know what's happening?

GG: Most situations in the world and in business are reasonably predictable. They tend to behave like honey, rather than sand.

If you take a spoonful of honey and you hold it up and let it drizzle down, it will slowly stream down in a steady flow and form a mound, a shallow cone that will gradually ease down until there's a flat surface. It's a process, and it's slow, predictable, with no catastrophic breaks or dynamics.

If you take grains of sand, though, and you pile them up, higher and higher, at some point there will be a landslide – a sudden, catastrophic shift.

The honey and the sand are two different types of system, and it's my belief that most systems are the first type. They're relatively slow and predictable. Nothing weird happens. A chair doesn't suddenly turn into a pink elephant. Certainly the natural world is predictable, ordered, lawful.

Now, it's obvious that, where people are involved, statistical relationships can suddenly change. For example, the markets may crash and the models that have been designed to track and forecast stock market movements will break down. But when it comes to models of consumer demand, these are much more like honey than sand.

You can imagine that the bottom might suddenly and spontaneously fall out of the tinned soup market, but it is extremely unlikely. Consumer habits move relatively slowly and the models that track this behaviour are very stable.

So when it comes to looking at the effects of marketing we are modelling a broadly predictable world, and the models seem to be useful enough to make us think we're on the right track.

Martian 2: But if your models are, in a sense, 'predicting the past' – if you're creating models that are refined until they fit tightly to the curve of past events, so that, given the same inputs, they'd produce the same outputs – doesn't that mean

that the only future you could accurately forecast is one that's the same as the past? Wouldn't your models only hold good for a future that included, say, a 9/11-type attack, followed by a disastrous tsunami three years later and a banking and financial crisis four years after that?

GG: If we go back to the honey-trickling image I was talking about, you actually find that the world does seem to tick along in a remarkably similar way, even when there are disturbances like this. It's bizarre.

Obviously, it is possible to imagine events that would be so earth-shattering that they would have a direct impact on, say, the UK sales of Kellogg's cornflakes. But they'd have to be big.

A world war would do it, but neither tsunamis in Asia nor major events closer to home, like the floods in Cumbria a couple of years ago, are likely to have hit cornflake sales across the UK as a whole. An event would have to be truly cataclysmic to abruptly upset the natural flow and balance of things, and you'd hardly be likely to overlook something on that sort of scale. You'd recognise it and make allowance for it in your models.

Martian 1: Do the results you get from your marketingQED models need to be interpreted? Or could a graduate trainee or an intern read them off just as competently as an experienced marketing director?

GG: Context is always important. A marketer familiar with the products being analysed, for example, could interpret them more easily than I could. If a model implied a certain price promotion was responsible for shifting 10 per cent of the year's volume, the marketer would know, far better than me, whether this was likely to be right. It is easy to interpret what the model says, but the marketer's ability to assess its accuracy will always be better than mine, simply because I don't know that business.

As I was saying before, you're always testing a broad hypothesis against the data. The way you know whether the hypothesis seems to be holding up or not is ultimately based on your feel for the market, your knowledge and experience of it.

If it happened that I was able to fit a model to the data that said that TV advertising campaigns and price had no impact at all on sales volume, and that all the fluctuations were caused only by competitor advertising and what the weather was doing, somebody looking at that who understood the business would say: 'I don't think so. That isn't right. That doesn't smell right to me.' You'd end up concluding that it was a spurious correlation, that you just happened, by coincidence, to be able to fit those factors to the data.

You're looking, obviously, for causes, rather than just correlations. It may be that there is some correlation, for example, between, say, shoe size and height. But even if that were true, you'd be pretty naïve to come out and announce that the one was causing the other. On the other hand, it's important to recognise that all statistics can do is give you correlations. Only a human can actually look at those and determine causality. You have to put your results through a human filter, a causality filter, to check that they're making sense. So if the statistics seemed to be saying 'Look, there's a correlation between the weather and competitive advertising and your sales,' you'd quickly decide that there must be other factors at work. You'd try another model which looked for correlations with a few other factors. And if that fitted the data better, then you'd know that you had got a better representation of reality.

The marketing director might look at what I saw as an unexpected bump in the data and say 'Oh yes. I know what that's about. That's because we had a big exhibition just then.'

That could be information that I, or any consultant who didn't know the industry, simply wouldn't be aware of. Without that insider knowledge, you'd end up with a model that didn't specifically take that exhibition out as a factor. And that would mean that the exhibition's impact would pollute and dilute the results of all the other factors in the model.

What the model is trying to do is fit, let's say, out-of-home or outdoor campaigns to the data you've got. So you'd see that out-of-home seemed to fit the data reasonably well, but not precisely, because of this spike, caused by the exhibition.

The problem would be that we were trying to account for the spike in terms of out-of-home advertising. What you need to be able to do is recognise that the spike is something else, work out what that something is and then put a separate variable into the next version of your model to take account of the exhibition.

When you do that, you find that the out-of-home data tightens up and gets better. It becomes a closer fit to the sales volumes you are trying to explain.

This is crucial stuff. However clever the statistical analysis is, being close to the road and knowing all the bumps and background is the key to getting better and better models. If you outsource the analysis, you're expecting someone else to make those decisions for you.

Martian 1: So the best marketing modelling in future will be done by marketers, not by modellers?

I think the best modelling is always going to be done right there, within the business. You need to be able to bring together two elements: the statistical knowhow and the knowledge of the business. The reason the businesses don't do it themselves is that the technical knowhow is seen as an insurmountable barrier. So they end up taking the other course of action and putting the analysis out – not nearly often enough, because of the cost – to the outside experts.

Given these considerations, the best approach is the exact opposite of that. The new strategy is to tool up the company's own staff so that they can handle the statistics themselves. That is the breakthrough that marketingQED has made. It is a completely new concept, giving mathematically untrained marketers powerful, affordable and usable statistical analysis, optimisation and forecasting software that they can easily run themselves on any PC.

Think of the thousands of options and choices you have within familiar desktop tools like Word or Excel. Now imagine analytical and forecasting software that was as easy to drive as Office and that let people in your marketing department do the kind of analysis that had previously been shipped out four times a year to the external statisticians. That's a change that rewrites the rules of the game.

It's so obvious. At least, it's so obvious to me now.

It wasn't that obvious before.

It was staring us in the face, and I couldn't see it. We were consultants. Like all consultants, everywhere, we believed we were doing a great job for our clients. The idea that we could equip ordinary people within their businesses to do it all themselves would have seemed preposterous to us as consultants.

But eventually we realised that they could do it, more often, more cheaply, more efficiently and with a better idea of what it might all mean. The question is no longer whether it can be done, but whether marketers want to get the benefits.

It turns out, of course, that everybody is interested in changing the way marketing mix decisions are analysed and monitored, and giving mere mortals the ability to run and refine models and make forecasts.

As consultants ourselves, we didn't know what we didn't know. We thought we were clever. We thought what was important was the statistics. But when we watched clients doing it, it really did become clear.

My colleague John Dawson went to do a meeting with a financial services company, a workshop with people from Germany and Austria. They imported the German data and then went through the model-building process together, iteratively, during the course of the day, putting it up on the screen at the front and asking 'What's this? What might account for this blip here and that spike there?'

'That's the ad campaign starting,' they said, 'and that's the Expo.'

So John was able to help build the model, with their knowledge, with the curve getting tighter and tighter to the sales line as they went through the process. Up till then, a firm of consultants had been providing this kind of data analysis service for them worldwide, with a staff of about 30 people in a sort of factory in America, constantly churning this stuff out and sending the results off to the branches in each country. The people in Germany would send off their data and eventually get this pack of documents back, which they couldn't make head nor tail of and which they didn't believe anyway, not least because they had no way of seeing where the answers had come from.

By contrast, John was able to stand in the room there with them and show them 'This is how the consultants must have got to that point,' recreating in a few hours what the US analysis factory had taken months to produce.

Together, the group in the room was able to add in factors that had been missed out, using the Germans' local knowledge to tighten it up and make the fit better and better. They then did the same exercise for Austria, and were feeling fairly pleased with themselves when someone said 'Wait, we've got some Italian data here, too.' They imported the data, stood back – and discovered they couldn't make any sense of what was going on. Nothing useful could be done, because there were no Italians in the room and no-one understood the Italian market for that product.

As John said afterwards, the difference it made was unmistakable. They were groping in the dark, because they had the data and a model that might have been a reasonable starting point, but there was nobody to say what assumptions might be valid under specifically Italian circumstances.

Martian 2: Let me ask you about the practicalities. How many variables and how many different types of data would typically go into one of these models?

GG: There's no limit. We have had one client who insisted on sticking 400 variables in. Normally, you would look at 20, maybe a maximum of 50.

They'd be factors like sales volume, price, distribution, price promotions, all your advertising spend – TV, radio, press and online – and sponsorship, sales force activities, competitor pricing, competitor advertising, weather, macroeconomic factors, like tsunamis and General Elections... The list can go on and on. Years ago, they used to put in a lot of factors like inflation, unemployment – and strikes, of course – but we don't tend to chase off up that alley so much now.

You're not trying to recreate or mimic reality exactly. All you're trying to get is a reasonably close approximation to it.

You want maybe 95 per cent of the variation accounted for. And the 80/20 rule tells you that 80 per cent of the variation is likely to be caused by 20 per cent of the variables. So you don't want to have to boil the ocean. You want to keep it pretty tight on the number of variables, to keep your data collection simple. In practice, too, the more variables you include, the more complicated it becomes to drive this hypothesis refinement process.

The other side of this is that if you are going to produce forecasts, you are going to have to produce a mini-forecast for every variable you have in the model.

You're going to have to say 'This is what the price will be. This is what we assume competitor advertising will be. This is what I expect the weather to be like.' All of this requires you to make assumptions about the future values of those elements to put into the model to drive your own sales forecast. You really don't want to bother putting in lots of elements that might have only a tiny impact. Quite frankly, the error on your estimates of what they will do will swamp any benefit you might get by putting them in.

Because of all this, it becomes fairly self-limiting. It becomes a question of looking at the top factors and forgetting the tail.

Some people might want to model the product at a national level and look at sales of a single product across the whole country – say, single cans of Diet Coke. Others maybe want to break it down and look at sales specifically in Tesco, or in a region, such as the North East. You may well be trying to slice and dice it in several different ways and several different dimensions. And there are people who are in a position to do that to a level way beyond what we are able to do.

Clive Humby of DunnHumby, who traditionally did all the analytics concerned with loyalty cards and customer data for Tesco, wrote a book about the techniques they devised. They could say, for example, 'We know when you bought cornflakes, because we know when you were in the store. So we know you were in that aisle at roughly that time, say, between 12 o'clock and 1 o'clock. And we also know we were running an advert there, on a big plasma screen TV, that you would have seen. And that there was a special promotion going on, with a special display gondola at the end of the aisle.' So they could start to marry up customer behaviour with very specific things that existed in specific retail stores at specific times.

Humby came and gave a very interesting talk when I was working at Accenture.

He told us, for example, that Tesco, which had its own credit card, had noticed that there were some customers who changed their credit cards every six months. They were credit card churners, switching cards all the time just to get the free deals, the 'free balance transfer for 6 months' offers. Tesco didn't want those people as credit card customers, so it worked out ways to avoid sending the application forms to them and made sure it only recruited people who habitually stuck with the same credit card for a long time.

What looks like dull data can help you piece together an awful lot of information about customers. There's the classic, much-quoted example of the customers, supposedly unearthed by the application of data mining, who'd buy the odd combination of beer and nappies. It may actually be an urban myth that there's a customer segment like this, but people are always talking about it. The idea is that the customer with a basket or trolley containing the odd mixture of beer and nappies is actually a harassed young father who has been sent out, perhaps in the middle of the night, for emergency supplies of Pampers. Finding himself in a big, almost empty supermarket, he gets the vital nappies and then rewards himself with a four-pack of beer for when he gets home.

Clive Humby was full of interesting stories like this, and DunnHumby are famous for their loyalty and basket analysis work.

But while you've got to admire the insights and expertise these niche specialists have developed, our mission, in our field, is to get our clients doing it for themselves. That's the key, the big breakthrough that we're offering the world.

Martian 1: Do you sell your desktop modelling and analytics software to the traditional econometrics consultancies, as well as marketers?

Yes, we do. They, of course, are the people who are best placed to recognise the technical strengths of the software.

Our credo, really, is quite simple. It comes down to two key points.

People should be analysing their data properly, modelling what has happened in the past and using their understanding of that to make specific and practical forecasts about what is likely to happen in the future and how their spending and decisions are likely to affect that.

They should be moving beyond relying on gut feel and the narrow experience that individual marketers can amass over the course of a career, and letting the data from thousands of transactions inform crucial business decisions.

But they should also be doing this with a full understanding of the context the business operates in. They should have tools at their fingertips that soon become familiar and that make this as easy for them as using Excel or PowerPoint.

Looking at these two points in a bit more detail, you could ask: 'What is the job of a marketer?' The answer has to be: 'To understand the customer.' So the question is, really, how you are going to go about trying to understand the customer better.

You are constantly trying to take the pulse of your customer and your markets. You are trying to get out there and see what works and what doesn't work, and you'll traditionally use a clutch of different methods to find out – surveys, focus groups, test marketing and so on. You'll get out there and talk to customers, pick up feedback from sales people and distributors, probably visit a few retailers. But these are all samples. They are methods that depend on taking a small numerical or geographical sample of your potential customer base and hoping it will accurately represent the whole.

By contrast, our modelling approach involves looking at the

whole knowledge set, the entire data set of everything that can be identified as bearing on sales up to this point. This is a method of trying to understand the customer by looking at what has happened in the past.

You have done stuff to the world. You have pulled levers and touched the world and you want to know, as exactly as you can, how it has responded.

Did your print campaign coincide with a sharp increase in sales? Good. But you still want to be able to tell whether it was that or the sudden change in the weather at the same time that altered the pattern of retail sales, or footfall in stores, or hits on your website. Your gut feel – it was a good campaign, you spent a lot and people liked the advertisement – is no substitute for being able to check, over repeated campaigns and repeated weather changes, whether it really is your advertising spend that's making the difference.

Relying on what the retailers tell you is not good enough. Relying on what customers tell you is just as bad. Customers don't always try to tell the truth. Even when they do, they may think one thing, but behave in a way that contradicts that. And even if their evidence was completely and consistently dependable, you'd still only be getting the messages from a small sample. Looking at the biggest possible picture, using all the data that tells you about people's actual behaviour, and finding ways to cross-check and analyse it correctly is the route that will ultimately give you the best chance of being able to accentuate the positive, eliminate the negative and, of course, avoid messing with Mister In-Between.

You want to be able to use all the evidence that's available to you, to mine the whole of your knowledge set, to use all the data.

Who could contest that? Who would ever be confident enough to say: 'Look, I can make a better forecast from the small data set I have accumulated from my career experience than you can make from looking at 100 per cent of the relevant data'?

Who would be arrogant enough to claim that they could hold that whole universe of data in their head and somehow, magically, analyse it more efficiently than was possible using advanced analytical and modelling techniques?

The world has moved on. We don't need to do the rituals and raindances any more. Today, we can use data instead of guesswork. We can isolate the factors that have shaped past performance and use that insight to plan future activities and investment.

Rational marketing needs a particular toolkit. A few years ago, it simply wasn't available. But now everything has changed. Memory is abundant, so we can store all the data we need. Computing power is limitless, so we can manipulate and analyse that data however we wish.

Now all we need is the courage and the software to do it regularly, routinely, at the coalface, in ways that will lead directly to better business decisions, better allocation of marketing resources and a bigger bang for every buck.

A F.A.S.T. Improvement in Stroke Awareness

An Institute of Practitioners in Advertising Effectiveness Awards gold winner

Stroke is the third biggest killer in Britain and the main cause of adult disability. It is cruel and arbitrary, striking out of the blue and hitting over 100,000 people a year, nearly half of whom die. Those left alive may recover, sometimes completely, but there are 300,000 people currently living with moderate or severe disabilities because of stroke.

Stroke occurs when the blood flow to the brain is stopped, either by a blood clot or, much more rarely, by a burst artery. Brain cells die quickly, and the key factor in saving those hit by stroke is the speed with which they can be treated, usually with clot-busting drugs, given intravenously.

For the more common 'ischaemic' strokes, the aim is to administer clot-busters within three hours. But the truth is, the faster the patient is treated, the more likely he or she is to survive and remain undamaged. In practice, every minute counts. And fast treatment depends on people – a friend, a spouse, even a grandchild – knowing when a stroke is occurring, knowing what to do and doing it as quickly as possible.

But ordinary people, and even doctors and other healthcare professionals, tend to be remarkably unaware of the symptoms of stroke and the importance of calling an ambulance straight away.

This was the background to the UK Department of Health's Stroke Awareness campaign, launched in February 2009. The objective was to save lives and reduce suffering and disability by teaching people what to look out for and how to react, with the help of a memorable acronym that had recently been developed by paramedics and the Stroke Association, a specialist charity.

The acronym was F.A.S.T., which stood for Face, Arms, Speech, Time to call 999. It was simple, concise and unforgettable. It provided a direct reminder of the three main symptoms of stroke – Facial drooping, Arm weakness and Speech slurring – plus immediate encouragement to treat the situation as an emergency and call an ambulance. And because it had been created by working paramedics, rather than ad agency copywriters, it had a credibility that was readily recognised and accepted by healthcare professionals.

Most strokes affect older people. Three quarters of sufferers are over 65, and this, in itself, meant that special attention had to be paid to the media and mechanics of putting the message across.

The campaign had to find ways to show, as well as explain, the telltale signs of stroke. It had to handle a serious and potentially frightening issue in a way that made people feel that their prompt action in making an emergency call could save a friend or loved one from death or disability. And it had to reach its core audiences of over-55s and people with existing health issues (including smoking, alcohol, blood pressure and cholesterol), while still speaking to health and social workers and to the general public.

Television and press were adopted as the main media, with long 40-second and 60-second commercials and larger print formats chosen to allow the information to be conveyed in a clear and measured way. But another key requirement for the campaign was a strong creative approach to communicating the core message.

The television executions revolved around the startling visual image of a fire breaking out in the brain, flickering and spreading as the victim's face sagged on one side, the arms went limp and the speech became slurred. Having led the viewer through the first three parts of the F.A.S.T. sequence, the ads then showed a phone and the instruction 'Time to call 999'.

But, significantly, the commercial didn't stop there. Once the call had been made, the burning hole in the victim's head started to 'heal itself', with the face moving back towards normality and the voiceover taking on an optimistic note as it delivered a positive final message: 'The faster you act, the more of the person you save.'

Print and online executions were closely based on the same elements, always featuring the 'fire in the brain' analogy and always ending with the line 'When stroke strikes, act F.A.S.T.'

The Act F.A.S.T. campaign began with two phases of advertising, in Feb/March 2009 and Nov/Dec 2009, followed by a smaller top-up wave in Feb/March 2010. The total investment in 2009 was £8.2 million, though, unusually, the figures that were released covered all-in costs, including production, research and agency fees, as well as media spend.

Qualitative research showed the impact of this activity was unmistakable. Viewers saw the TV ads and remembered them. Some found them disturbing, but they were unquestionably hard-hitting, informative and empowering. *Marketing* magazine rated the commercials as having the highest cut-through and percentage recall rates of any government advertising in recent years.

Almost immediately, evidence began to emerge that seemed to indicate the campaign was changing people's behaviour out in the real world. Health authorities reported that the number of victims arriving in hospital stroke units within three hours had begun to climb.

But there could have been other reasons for this, and it needed careful checking and modelling to exclude other possible explanations for the increase. There had been no sudden upsurge in the number of strokes or in the total number of 999 emergency calls. No prominent celebrity had suffered a stroke that would have prompted extra news coverage since the TV gardener Monty Don in April 2008, and there had been no other television or press campaigns about stroke that could have affected the statistics.

Throughout 2009, almost 10,000 stroke sufferers were identified as having got to a hospital stroke unit quicker and having been able to benefit from modern clot-busting (thrombolysis) techniques. Once other factors had been ruled out, it was clear that this improvement was attributable to the F.A.S.T. campaign. Lives had been saved, disabilities had been prevented, and common sense indicated that the vast majority of these victims must be better off than they would otherwise have been.

But modern medicine and scientific marketing demand a more studied examination of costs and benefits than this.

NICE, the National Institute for Health and Clinical Excellence, judges the economic benefits of medical treatments in terms of QALYs – quality-adjusted life years. A QALY represents a year of life of reasonable quality and is priced at £30,000. This figure is multiplied by a value between 1.0 (perfect health) and 0.0 (death), with intermediate values reflecting disabilities or impaired health, in order to place a cash value on the benefits to be gained as a result of a treatment or intervention.

Crunching the QALY numbers for the F.A.S.T. campaign (after allowing for the extra care costs for the survivors with disabilities who would otherwise have died), the Department of Health calculated a payback of £25.9 million in 2009 for its £8.2 million spend. In other words, the immediate net gain to society for every £1 spent on the campaign was £3.50.

This figure is clearly only part of the story, though, as it is based only on the benefits delivered by fast access to thrombolysis in specialist stroke units. It gives no credit for the thousands of other patients whose outcomes will have been improved simply by getting to a hospital quicker. And, of course, it does not begin to capture the long-term payoffs of a successful public education campaign.

Millions of Britons who would not have recognised the symptoms of stroke have now been taught what to look for and how to react. That is knowledge that will be carried forward and could still be saving lives in decades to come.

For the moment, though, modelling has been used to forecast the value that will be generated over three years of the F.A.S.T. campaign. The model that has been developed reflects the relationships between marketing spend, campaign awareness levels and 999 call volumes, and it predicts a return on marketing investment (ROMI) over the full three years of almost 5:1, making this one of the most cost-effective public awareness campaigns ever.

'Shall I refuse my dinner because I do not fully understand the process of digestion?'
– Oliver Heaviside

CHAPTER 10

Modelling 101

Explaining the past, exploring the present, exploiting future potential – analytics replaces guesses with real numbers. Elasticities, regression analysis and R^2 may sound daunting, but desktop modelling makes pro techniques easily available to all.

What is modelling?

Most marketing decisions – for the last hundred years or more – have been taken by soothsayers, astrologers and alchemists. Or, if they haven't, they might as well have been.

Experience, intuition and guesswork have been honoured and valued beyond everything, for the simple reason that there was little else on which to base decision making.

Firms could look at their sales histories and praise and promote those senior marketers who had been in charge during periods of growth. But, in general, companies have not had accurate ways of measuring the payback on their marketing communications, knowing what they could have done better or even assessing whether their marketing budgets could have been spent more effectively.

This raindance culture – in which so little is truly known

about the causal links between marketing activities and sales performance – has a superstitious basis that appears primitive alongside the other business disciplines that have been developed and studied so intensively in the last 50 years.

Compare the guesses, assumptions and approximations that underpin normal marketing practice with the strictly numerate rigour of, say, the Six Sigma approach to process quality, with its aim of a maximum defect rate of 3.4 per million.

Marketers do what they've always done, adding the odd extra here and there based on what they've seen work for other people or have read about in books or online. They follow ritual procedures, the origins of which are lost in the mists of time.

They dance their dance and they chant their chants. And then, because there's nothing much else they can do, they wait and scan the sky anxiously, looking for the first little cloud that will bring with it the promise of rain.

Modelling is unique in providing an approach that marketers can use to tell them just how cost effective their past marketing communications activities were – and how their future budgets might be spent more wisely. This is a form of quantitative research that sucks up vast, shapeless masses of data and turns that raw data into information that can be acted on and used to improve key marketing decisions.

The science of modelling is not new. In the UK, it has been used by a select group of large and well-funded companies for more than 30 years, though the relevant methodologies of measurement, analysis and forecasting were already being developed decades before that.

But the cost and delays associated with modelling projects carried out by external consultants have restricted its use to a few big international brands. Insights of this kind have not generally been brought to bear on the real-time problems and questions facing ordinary marketers in ordinary companies.

Britain's Institute of Practitioners in Advertising summed up the situation succinctly several years ago. Referring to econometrics, probably the most commonly used type of modelling, the industry body recognised the untapped potential:

'To most people, econometrics is an obscure and intimidating art, practised by ivory-tower boffins, with little relevance to the day-to-day practice of marketing,' said the IPA.

'We believe that this lack of understanding is preventing UK clients and their agencies from exploiting the full potential of econometrics.'

What's in it for me?

Modelling offers two main payoffs for marketers. It can explain a brand's past sales performance and it can provide practical tools with which to test hypotheses and explore future options.

Many companies jump to conclusions about the connections between past marketing activity and the sales volumes that were seen at the time the activity was going on.

Myths arise – and, of course, some senior marketers will often be keen to promote the idea that it was their shrewd, inspired campaigns that made sales happen, rather than the feelgood factor around a royal wedding, a burst of sunny summer weather or the economic boost provided by tax cuts.

Wrongly assigning responsibility and credit for past success is a surefire way of getting it wrong in future, so there is a direct business benefit in knowing what really determined past performance. Knowing the truth is worth money in the bank.

In practice, modelling in marketing is largely about defining the relatively small number of key factors that genuinely influence sales.

These will include some factors that are under the marketer's control, such as promotions, price and advertising campaigns, and others – from competitor activity to seasonal factors and macro-economic shifts – that are emphatically not. As this work continues, seasonal influences can be isolated and allowed for and one-off events and incidents that affect sales can be broken out and investigated.

Once these influences are identified, econometric analysis can start to pick apart and quantify their individual and separate effects, measuring, for example, the sales response per unit of TV advertising activity or the impact of a one-degree rise in temperature.

These are vital figures. If you know the sales response generated by each unit of activity, you can calculate the overall impact of your activity and its specific contribution to profits. You can also, crucially, use this knowledge to make useful and informed predictions about how sales would behave under various different assumptions and scenarios.

Fig 9 shows how two and a half years' weekly sales data, once modelled, can be decomposed into the incremental sales resulting from each of the main types of marketing activity over that period. Each layer of the total sales cake is the sales due to one marketing variable. You can see the effect of TV advertising, for example, as the dark grey layer. Radio's sales are represented by two striped bursts and sales due to online campaigns are the white icing on the cake.

Fig 9. The cake and the icing: the components of sales success can be isolated

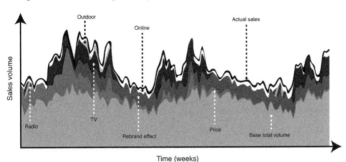

Using modelling, you can go further than this and 'test drive' different scenarios. What effect would spending an extra £1 million on TV advertising have? How would that compare with investing the same money in tactical price promotions at the point of sale? Would an overall price reduction generate higher profits by boosting volume for years to come?

Answers based on your own data

These are the kind of questions that have always been difficult, if not impossible, for marketers to answer with any degree of certainty. In the past, the only guides have been the folk wisdom of the marketing community and the relatively small amount of experience any one marketer could accumulate in the course of a career.

Modelling can provide answers based on the evidence of thousands of actual data points. It is still possible to get the interpretations wrong, of course, but the injection of facts into the analysis is at least likely to get rid of people's cherished misconceptions.

Modelling provides excellent tools for measuring and analysing the short and medium-term effects of marketing activity, including payback, the relative impact of different campaigns and the coverage and frequency levels needed to make messages stick or reach specific sales targets.

It can help marketers decide what media mix to use, whether to use burst campaigns or a slow, steady drip, how soon to follow up after the last activity and whether to emphasise or avoid particular times of the year.

It can help shed light on many of the subtler and more elusive impacts of marketing activity, such as cross-brand interactions within a portfolio, umbrella effects and halo effects. It can even allow you to look at impacts in a competitive context, enabling you, for example, to calculate how much advertising would be needed to offset the effects of a competitor's activity.

And although most people tend to think of modelling as being concerned mainly with relating marketing activity to sales, the same techniques can be used to examine non-sales measures like the effects of marketing on distribution, brand awareness or call centre enquiry volumes.

No magic wand

This is a huge and exciting range of possibilities. But marketers need to be aware that there are some general limitations on when and how modelling can be used to good effect. For example, it is at its best and most useful when it helps to disentangle multiple effects that are superimposed on each other. But sometimes the picture is too simple to produce revealing results. If there is too little information (in particular, variation) in the historic dataset that is being used, it may be virtually impossible to isolate individual effects.

If two factors always vary at the same time and in the same proportions, never breaking step with each other, there is simply no opportunity to separate out their individual effects.

Sales of Christmas puddings tend to peak at a predictable time of year, so that is a market that exhibits exaggerated seasonality. Advertising for Christmas puddings also, naturally enough, peaks at exactly the same time of year. If the same weight of advertising is deployed at the same time each year and produces a very similar sales curve each Christmas, it becomes hard indeed to separate out the advertising from the seasonality. Introducing occasional variations in advertising weight would make this separation a great deal easier and more reliable, possibly revealing, for instance, that the pudding manufacturer could halve its advertising budget and still sell almost as many puddings, simply on the basis of the underlying seasonal demand.

In the same way, if an advertiser uses two creative executions but they are always split in exactly the same proportions, it is difficult to break out any useful information about their individual effects. The scope for analysis and modelling is far greater if the historical data exhibits variation that can provide discrete information about the performance of each execution.

The models we use for marketing purposes are developed from the historic time-series data that reflects actual sales, marketing activity, price changes, seasonality and similar factors. Like all mathematical models, they are equations. On one side of the equation, there is, usually, sales (the *dependent variable*). On the other side, there is the range of explanatory factors that may be responsible for causing variations in sales volumes.

These factors are known, technically, as the *independent variables*. There are normally just a handful of these, but sometimes, usually ill-advisedly, clients may insist on 40 or more. Deciding which explanatory factors should be included (and how few are actually necessary and relevant) forms a key part of any modelling project.

The modelling process attaches weights (known as *coefficients*) to each of the chosen explanatory factors. From these weights, it is possible to calculate the useful figure known as *elasticity* which, roughly speaking, is just a number that specifies how sales will react to a 1 per cent change in each factor. For example, if your price elasticity is 'minus 3', that means a 1 per cent increase in price will lead to approximately a 3 per cent drop in sales volume. Incidentally, 'minus 3' isn't a bad starting point as an estimate of price elasticity for most branded consumer products. When you are looking at broader product categories, they tend to be around 'minus 1', as a category will generally be less sensitive to price changes than a particular branded product.

The statistician is trying to replicate the sales patterns shown in the historical data by determining which factors are relevant and assigning appropriate weights to them. If this is done successfully, the sales fluctuations that occurred in the real world will be closely matched by the 'best fit' line predicted by the model.

This 'best fit' line is generally determined using regression analysis. This is a basic statistical technique that fits a line through the scatter of data points in such a way that it minimises the sum of the distances between the line and the data points (actually, squared distances are used, for technical reasons, but we don't need to go into that now).

Once the best fit line has been generated, values can be read off it for intermediate points and it becomes possible to extrapolate the line forward to provide predictions for the future.

Modelling for the other 90 per cent

In the past, it has always taken a lot of time and effort to produce models – and this has been reflected in the cost. Three months has been regarded as quite good going, and a £100,000 bill would not be at all unusual.

This is obviously a good investment if it substantially improves the performance of a brand and the marketing impact that can be generated from a particular budget.

If it just leads to a set of reports that are read and filed away without changing what people do or producing any tangible improvements, it is a monumental waste of resources and cash.

High-level expertise is expensive and even the most qualified and experienced specialists cannot construct useful models without large volumes of data (usually at least two years' detailed records) and a good deal of background knowledge of market factors like the relevant competitors, trends and legislation. This industry context will probably have to be pieced together from conversations with the marketing team and examination of previous market research.

It is unlikely that the modeller will have a close personal knowledge of the characteristics of the particular market or industry involved, so the briefing process is vitally important and needs to include the setting of specific, explicit objectives and priorities.

This is the way of working we have become used to, at least among the big brands, over the past 20 or 30 years.

But one of the reasons I am so excited by the development of the new generation of desktop analysis and modelling software is that this has the potential to completely disrupt the traditional model. Where money, time and statistical expertise were all needed to bring modelling to bear on marketing problems, the desktop software – no harder to master than Microsoft Office products like Excel or PowerPoint – makes powerful modelling and analysis facilities available to many more people.

The cost of acquiring this software and using it for a full year in a marketing department is likely to be around half the cost of a single, one-off snapshot report prepared by an outside consultancy.

In return for this relatively minor investment, marketers can gain direct access to analytics and modelling tools that are genuinely on a par with those available to the specialist consultancies. All the fundamental statistical expertise that is needed to interrogate and manipulate the data, create and validate models, produce valuable business insights, generate predictions and test drive alternative scenarios for the future is embedded in the software.

And the time needed to carry out these operations, once the relevant data has been collected, checked and collated, is reduced to minutes, rather than months.

This is important in itself, as the results of any modelling exercise have a limited shelf life.

Modellers usually talk in terms of an update every 12 months. But as the data gets older and new products are introduced, new campaigns are rolled out and economic circumstances change, any model steadily becomes less accurate in its ability to reflect the outside world. If you have to wait for an annual update and it then takes two or three months to produce any results, you are automatically going to be spending most of your time working with obsolete information.

Even if the results produced almost immediately by the desktop modelling software were not intrinsically as good as those emanating from the £100,000 consultancy project – and there is no reason at all to suppose that to be true – the fact that they were up to date would be a strong recommendation.

Suddenly, the 90 per cent of marketers who have been excluded from using modelling by cost and time considerations are able to support their decisions with factual evidence derived from the past performance of their brands and campaigns. They can apply modelling, quickly and routinely, to help them make the most of the day-to-day opportunities and defuse the budget and resource allocation problems that crop up in every marketing department.

Blending modelling with marketing insight

Once marketers become fully familiar with the toolkit that desktop modelling software places at their disposal, they will be able to produce 'home-grown' analysis and models that are as good as – or sometimes actually better than – those that the big brands get from calling in the external modellers. For all their technical expertise, these outsiders are seldom going to have the feel for a market, a sector or a territory that comes with working in an area day in and day out.

A good marketer who has to work without the benefit of modelling is, inevitably, flying blind.

It may not feel conspicuously odd or unusual, though, because that is probably how he or she will have had to operate throughout a whole career. Compared with another marketer, working on a big brand for a big company and aided by external consultants' reports, he or she will necessarily be at a disadvantage.

But with the advent of desktop modelling software, access to data-driven analysis is democratised. If the people responsible for big brands are slow to react and change their approach, they will actually be overtaken by those who learn to apply the new tools in conjunction with their own intimate knowledge of the marketplace.

A bad model is worse than no model at all. A bad model will inspire a misplaced sense of confidence that could lead to very expensive mistakes. So what makes a good model, in the marketing context?

A good model should fit the data and be statistically valid, unbiased and accurate enough for the context in which it is to be used.

As far as fitting the data is concerned, there are many measures of model quality. One well-known, though far from perfect, measure is R-Squared. This is a figure, in the range of 0 to 1, that measures the proportion of the movement in sales (or whatever else is being charted) that is captured or explained by your model.

An R^2 of 1 means the model is impossibly perfect and accounts for every twitch in the historic time series. An R^2 of 0 means that whoever invested their time and effort in the work has managed to achieve a model that explains absolutely nothing.

Non-specialists tend to like R^2 because it seems simple and intuitive. The higher the figure, the better. If $R^2 = 0.96$ – often expressed as a percentage, 96 per cent – that certainly sounds like a pretty good fit.

In practice, an R^2 of 0.9 is common if the series involved is reasonably stable. If the past results are more erratic, an R^2 of 0.7 (meaning that 70 per cent of the variation is explained by the model) may be the best you can do.

Another measure – estimated standard error – gives the average error for the model as a whole, which means it can be used, for example, in calculations of confidence intervals in predictions and simulations.

Getting away from the theory, one practical approach is to verify the accuracy of the model by making it come up with predictions for an out-of-sample period. If you had data for three years, for example, you might use the figures for the first 30 months in building the model. You would hold back the most recent half-year's data and then road test the model against this to see how closely its predictions matched what had actually happened in the last six months. Conducting this kind of exercise – known as a hold-out test – allows you to check that your mathematical model is generating a reliable representation of the real world.

Statistical validity is a critical matter but it can be assured by careful use of validation diagnostics within a properly thought-out software package. In the same way, technical tools are available that sniff out bias arising from missing factors or the inclusion of spurious factors by spotting characteristic patterns in the errors (the gaps between the actual results and the model's predictions). For example, a long-term upward trend in the errors might signal that a key factor like the effect of price changes or the impact of competitive advertising has been left out.

Above all, however, the single most important quality underpinning a good model is that it should reflect the real world and not fly in the face of common sense. And the best people to judge that are the marketers.

Information you can act on

If modelling is to deliver tangible and profitable results, the information that emerges from such projects needs to be clear, relevant and understood. That hasn't always been the case in the past, and some modellers have been guilty of regarding their job as done before their clients have understood enough to take action.

For example, though elasticities mean a lot to the statisticians, marketing people may have trouble getting their heads round them and tuning in to their significance. For the marketer who is not used to thinking in those terms, it is not necessarily simple at all to take such ideas on board and make good use of them.

Another way of delivering the punchline may be as effects per unit of input. A one-degree drop in temperature might boost fuel oil sales by 2.5 per cent. One hundred TV ratings might lift car insurance sales by 5 per cent.

Relationships like this can be embedded in spreadsheets or used in simulation software to allow the marketers to experiment for themselves and test drive the effects of different courses of action. They can adjust the inputs to see how sales would rise or fall and then to see the effect this would have on profitability.

As long as the marketers can come up with realistic assumptions about the future behaviour of the main factors that affect sales, the model can be used to generate forecasts. These can then be tweaked to reflect different strategies involving different budget allocations, media weights, pricing policies and promotions.

At its simplest, though, the model can be used to isolate, explore and quantify the contribution made by a single factor – either an external one, like temperature, or marketing activity, such as an online campaign or a pricing change.

Marketers can see the difference it would have made to past sales if an advertising campaign had been run with twice the budget, or not run at all. And they can use the model to peer into the future and take vital decisions about resource allocation that are based on evidence-based predictions, rather than gut feel and guesswork.

Marketing's long-standing culture of raindancing, with its confusing tapestry of traditions and beliefs, habits and assumptions, hunches and old wives' tales, is not fit for purpose in a world where big brands can be shown to waste millions every year and smaller companies simply have no way of basing their decisions on fact.

The idea that 'rational marketing' should be a new and radical concept would be funny, if it wasn't so sad.

But we are so used to marketing decisions driven by emotion

and the kind of spot diagnosis that stems from narrow personal experience that data-driven decision-making sounds like a potentially dangerous novelty.

I am an analyst and, in this context, an activist. But even I am not saying that key marketing decisions should be handed over, lock, stock and barrel, to be dictated entirely by the output from a desktop modelling package.

What I am saying is that choosing blind guesswork and ignoring the information potentially provided by many thousands of data points is wilfully perverse. Data-driven decision-making may be a step too far, but who could argue against data-informed decision-making? How can darkness be better than light?

In Robert Shaw and David Merrick's influential book *Marketing Payback*, there is an interesting case study that looks at Kraft's conversion to analytic modelling. Before it started to take this issue seriously, Kraft was getting many of its marketing resource allocation decisions badly – and expensively – wrong.

It was the world's second largest food company, with a vast range of long-established international brands. Yet it discovered that the products that were essential for its future were not receiving the marketing support and investment they needed. In the usual mix of false assumptions, portfolio politics and unsupported guesswork, the key brands that were responsible for over 80 per cent of Kraft's growth were getting just 20 per cent of the group's marketing budget.

Tom Lloyd, Kraft's marketing analytics guru for ten years, oversaw big changes in the way the company used data to support its resource allocation decisions. He told Shaw and Merrick that the new emphasis on modelling had major strategic implications.

'This is not merely an exercise in justifying expenditure,' Lloyd said. 'It is a vital element in staying ahead in the competitive game.'

That comment was made in 2005. While Kraft had already taken steps to raise its game by then, it is shocking how many others still have not seen the light, nearly eight years later.

Few other companies will ever have the opportunity to misplace marketing resources on that scale. Even fewer will be able to spend as much on econometric analysis and modelling as Kraft did once it recognised the error of its ways. But that kind of abrupt turnaround should no longer be necessary. Nobody these days needs to be starting from scratch. Now that affordable, sophisticated and usable desktop software is becoming available for individual marketers and departments, modelling is on its way to becoming part of the day-to-day armoury of every ambitious marketer and every company that cares about making the most of its marketing money.

'The only source of knowledge is experience'
– Albert Einstein

CHAPTER 11

Tales from the Front Line

Why most industries regularly and systematically overspend within their favourite media channels. And how analytics helps the UK Department of Health count the QALYs and get value for money.

I know I will have already shocked a lot of people with the blunt declaration that four out of five companies systematically *underspend* on their marketing campaigns, stopping too soon and wasting straightforward profit opportunities.

Now I want to draw your attention to the equally disturbing fact that almost every major marketing operation also wastes resources in the opposite direction, by *overspending*, in a particular and clearly identifiable way.

Every industry seems to have its own favourite, dominant form of marketing activity, and the companies within that sector will all tend to overemphasise and overspend on this.

In the pharmaceuticals industry, for example, the emphasis has always been on the sales force. The pharmaceutical sales people go out and visit doctors to talk to them, explain new drugs to them and fill them in on the scientific background, in a broadly educational way. It's to do with information, credibility and building trusting relationships, and it's necessarily very labour-intensive.

By contrast the consumer packaged goods companies – Kellogg's, Cadbury, Nestlé and the rest – typically use TV commercials, backed up with a lot of price promotions in supermarkets. In the past, there would have been even more television advertising, but since the 1990s, the emphasis has shifted much more towards price promotions as the best way to influence buying decisions right there at the point of sale.

If you think about it, you can usually get a money-off deal of one sort or another on any day-to-day supermarket product you want to buy. In any product category, there'll be at least one brand on special offer on any given day. But the shopper who wants to take advantage of this must be prepared to switch brands, to drop any idea of brand loyalty. And, of course, that is the point of these promotions, to unhook people from their habitual purchasing patterns and persuade them to come over to your brand by offering them an eye-catchingly low price. There's a downside to this as a tactic, though. The new customers who come to you because of a short-term price deal are highly likely to revert to the brand they would normally buy as soon as your promotion is over and the price goes back to its usual level. And the manufacturers' nightmare – though not the supermarkets' – is a race to the bottom, where tit-for-tat price promotions drive prices down to levels where suppliers' profit margins just evaporate.

It's one of those game theory things. Once I do it, you have to retaliate in kind. To some extent, you can see that the manufacturers have shot themselves in the foot, as this all results in goods being sold at prices that are lower than consumers would be prepared to pay.

It takes a very strong and confident company to defy the

conventions of the sector and take the risk of adopting a different approach.

Apart from anything else, it's not just the marketers who have developed habits and assumptions about the way price promotions should be used. Shoppers learn from what they see around them, and they now have expectations that they should be able to buy foods, cleaning materials, alcoholic drinks and all kinds of household basics at aggressively low prices, just by being prepared to ditch or suspend their brand loyalties. Some price-conscious consumers will leave the supermarket without buying some of the items on their shopping lists, deferring purchases for days or weeks until they can get the bargains they seek.

But if pharma is dominated by sales force activity and consumer packaged goods sales are largely driven by price promotions, there are other product categories where old-fashioned print advertising still holds sway. Consumer electronics may be a sector that's characterised by fads and features and short-lived, fast-changing product ranges, but it still tends to favour print. National and local newspapers still carry double page spreads showing dozens of different laptops and tablets, mobiles and mp3 players, satnavs, games consoles and flat-screen televisions. Inserts in magazines are used a lot, while point of sale material tends to be based on magazine-type colour catalogues and many companies mail out circulars to talk to potential customers in their homes. These high-tech electronic products are energetically promoted online, of course, yet print is still a major part of the marketing mix.

Financial services organisations – banks, insurers, credit card companies and investment firms – have always favoured direct mail. They like to be able to know exactly who their offers have gone to and to be able to trace exactly what response they're getting from each market segment and each burst of marketing activity. As digital printing equipment has improved, they've got very excited in the last few years about the possibilities offered by 'transpromo', the technique of printing highly individualised full colour marketing material onto millions of monthly or quarterly bills and statements that customers cannot avoid opening and reading.

So different industries use different tactics. And it's rare for any one marketing operation to even consider utilising the whole range of possibilities that make up the marketing armoury.

Marketers tend to focus quite narrowly on a small number of techniques and variables that they think work best in their industries. They have their tried and tested methods – but they're usually a lot more tried than tested.

Objective testing might well reveal that these people are using what they're used to, rather than what would work best and provide the best returns. They have their old favourites – 'Well, we always do TV in this industry' – but the basis for sticking with them may never have been thoroughly examined.

I remember looking at the results of modelling projects across multiple industries around the world and noticing an amazing pattern.

It seemed that every major marketing organisation, virtually without exception, was habitually overspending on its dominant media vehicle. People would spend in their strongest medium until they had achieved saturation in the market place. And they would then go right ahead and spend some more, even though that money could be shown to bring better returns elsewhere.

I have seen it happen time and time again, to the point where

I almost consider it a universal truth – and there aren't many of those in marketing.

So, if you're in financial services, I can tell you straight away, before we even look at any data, that you are highly likely to be overspending on direct mail.

If you're in consumer goods, you are throwing money away by going to the well too often on price promotions.

And in pharmaceuticals, the area where I cut my analytical teeth, companies famously spend far too much on their sales forces. In fact, it was using modelling that allowed me to help pharma companies rein in the overspending on their sales teams and switch the spend to other, more responsive marketing vehicles.

I remember being asked to give a speech at a conference in Amsterdam in 2004 on the subject of return on investment in the pharma industry.

I showed my audience response curves that illustrated the relationship between the number of people in a sales force and total sales, for several different companies where we had been given access to the data and done the analysis. Company after company showed the same pattern – they were all sitting right up there on the flat part of the response curve. They were overspending, in what I identified as the industry's equivalent of the Cold War arms race.

What happened was that Company A would send its reps in to talk to the GPs and hospital doctors and see a noticeable uplift in its sales in that area. Company B would then hire more reps and send them in to talk to the doctors. They would then get into a process of effectively outbidding each other, inflating the number of sales calls, the number of reps in the field and the costs of putting them out there. As in the post-war nuclear arms race, this produced a ridiculous level of overkill capacity, and it guaranteed that the companies on both sides would see their profitability drain away.

Because of this, it was clear to me that the first major pharmaceutical company to break ranks, defy the industry's conventions and switch money across into other marketing channels and vehicles could potentially reap impressive rewards.

A year after the Amsterdam conference, one of the industry giants took the plunge and did it. Pfizer made a very bold move, trimming back its sales forces in several key markets and moving its marketing investment money across into other activities.

As it turned out, there were lots of other ways the company could get its messages and information across to doctors. Running conferences, organising specialist seminars and setting up brief, well-targeted lunchtime meetings for doctors in hospitals were just a few of the initiatives that were introduced, funded by the savings made in the sales force. Pfizer launched advocacy programmes, key opinion leader programmes and even direct mail campaigns, just to move away from the flattened top of the response curve and get real value for the last slice of the money it was spending.

Our analysis had shown us that those other marketing investment opportunities were being underexploited while the rest of the industry played follow-my-leader and stuck to the conventional wisdom that the sales force was the only lever that mattered. When Pfizer grasped the nettle and changed its approach, the positive results showed that the tale the response curve told was not just a matter of theory but a clear pointer to better performance and an improved ROI.

I have also had some interesting experiences on the other side of the healthcare industry, working with the UK Department of Health. This gave me unexpected insights into how government really works and how public sector marketing methods and objectives compare with those in the private sector.

One new technique was agent-based modelling – a relatively new form of modelling that, as far as I know, has yet to be put to widespread use as a business tool. It's based on the idea of creating a sort of Sim City, a simulated society and population, in a computer model, that you can then experiment with. You can create a series of rules and watch how the people and the influences on them – word of mouth, marketing, cultural background, beliefs and so on – interact with each other. You can run experiments and see what plays out, to help you predict more accurately what might happen in a real population.

I worked on a broad range of consultancy projects for the Department of Health, and there were some fairly sophisticated agent-based modelling projects going on there at that time. In the area of sexual health, for example, the DH was using this kind of modelling to investigate behavioural interactions among teenagers, such as how STIs (sexually transmitted infections) might spread, and even, oddly enough, how the pattern of teenage pregnancies might work out among a population.

Within a particular population, it's not actually true that there is no relation between one pregnancy and another. In clusters of friends and groups of younger teenagers, for example, the occurrence of one pregnancy within the group sharply inhibits the likelihood of another one occurring, at least for a time. That's not surprising. The first pregnancy comes as a clear warning to others in the group of the necessity for changes of behaviour or birth control methods.

When you are setting up the agent-based modelling process for something like a sexually transmitted disease, you introduce rules like, for example, 'People will sleep with a new partner after x days (or weeks, or months)', 'Relationships will last an average of y months' and 'After the end of a relationship, people will find another sexual partner in an average of z weeks.' Then you can set the model in motion and observe the rate and pattern of the spread of the disease through the population.

The next step is to add in new rules to represent the effects of policy changes like better sex education in schools or giving out free condoms and see what impact these would have. This can provide a basis for quite interesting predictions. It might show, for instance, that after a certain time the prevalence of the disease within the population would stabilise and top out at, say, 15 or 20 per cent.

For the Department of Health, one important objective of these agent-based modelling projects was to understand and forecast the effectiveness of public health awareness campaigns. But the powers that be were not prepared to rely on just one approach to understanding behavioural interactions, and that was why I had become involved, bringing with me my marketing analytics toolkit.

I soon found myself working across the full range of DH marketing campaigns. The total marketing spend was £120 million a year, so it was important to know what was working. My main task was to analyse the effectiveness of the campaigns and, by extension, the value for money they were delivering.

Most of these campaigns dealt with familiar public health issues, such as sexual health, teenage pregnancies, cigarette smoking, drugs and alcohol harm. Others were less traditional, like the Change4Life campaign, which focused on educating and raising awareness of healthy eating and regular exercise among children and their families, with the aim of reducing the incidence of unhealthy weight gain in children and promoting longer life.

I had become involved with the DH in autumn 2009 and I worked with the department for nine months, two or three days a week, and gathered a lot of detailed, useful information. Some of the analysis – for example, of the smoking campaign – did show a positive return on the money invested. The smoking campaign showed a clear positive return, with a £2.07 payback over one year for every pound that was spent, and its success was eventually recognised with an IPA Advertising Effectiveness Silver Award.

The percentage of smokers in the overall population had been declining, in fits and starts, since the 1960s, when something like two thirds of the population smoked. The figures had come down and down, leaving roughly 22 per cent of adults, almost exclusively in the 'routine and manual workers' group, with a fairly fixed and intractable smoking habit. Gordon Brown's administration decreed that more needed to be done to bring the smoking rate down to less than 21 per cent.

The civil service responded to this target with a range of marketing communications to increase awareness, change attitudes and ultimately encourage actual changes in behaviour.

Within the routine and manual workers category, the prevalence of smoking was much higher – something like 28 per cent – and the government really wanted to get that figure down as quickly as possible. But there was a core of hard-to-reach people with little or no intention of giving up smoking, who would need a particular effort.

So the civil servants were focused on two Key Performance Indicators, which involved getting the overall smoking rate down to 21 per cent and the hard-to-reach group's rate down to 25 per cent. Various outdoor campaigns had been tried, without a great deal of success in terms of actual behaviour change, but one initiative that was beginning to have a real impact was the introduction of the Quit Kit packs.

This simple kit – basically a box of information and tools to help the smoker to give up – was incredibly successful. We could measure how the offline advertising drove people to the campaign website and the telephone hotlines and watch the take-up of Quit Kits go through the roof. We could track how many people started trying to quit smoking and make accurate estimates of how many of those would succeed and end up breaking free of the habit.

The stats show that people who manage to give up for a year are quite unlikely to go back to it, but that most smokers have to try many times before they manage to quit. They typically make an effort and go through the worst part, the first two or three weeks, and then lapse back into it. So the campaign line that was adopted was unheroic, but realistic. 'Never give up giving up' was not the world's most uplifting and inspiring slogan. But it chimed with the grim reality facing addicted smokers who knew it would be better for them if they could free themselves from their burden. And the campaign around the Quit Kit did seem to help a lot of people take the first steps.

Once we knew how many people were encouraged to start the process of quitting, we could start to work out what the cash value of the campaign was, in terms of savings for the health service. If you estimated the amount saved on not having to treat smoking-related illnesses and related that back to the spend on the advertising and Quit Kit packs, you could actually come up with a reasonably robust ROI figure for the whole campaign.

I was engaged in this long project as a specialist in marketing effectiveness, rather than specifically as an econometrician, and most of this work used more conventional market research-type inputs. But I did carry out some modelling on the tobacco data, to show how the marketing drove people to the website and the call centres. I even ended up doing a public presentation on the smoking campaign in a big public forum run by the Central Office of Information.

Besides the smoking campaign, one of the others that was able to demonstrate a strong positive ROI was the information campaign about strokes. This won an Institute of Practitioners in Advertising Effectiveness Award [*see case study, p159*], but it was the ability to prove that it was effective and could justify itself in cost terms that mattered more to the Department of Health. The advertising campaign showed people who were displaying stroke symptoms, such as paralysis of one side of the face, inability to raise an arm or slurred speech. The acronym deployed to drive education and behavioural recall was F.A.S.T. – Face, Arm, Speech, Time (to call 999). It was graphically arresting, and used the analogy of part of the head burning and being consumed by flames to encourage people to act quickly.

The impetus behind this campaign was the recognition that fast treatment, within three hours of the onset of a stroke, could go a long way towards minimising the damage and after-effects and preserving brain function that would otherwise be lost.

As part of my work on this, I was able to compare the number of stroke victims calling 999 during the campaign with the number doing so in an earlier sample period. That gave us a picture of the uplift generated by the campaign. We could assign a value to a complete recovery and another to a partial recovery with lessened long-term damage, do the sums and come up with a cash figure for the savings, which could then be compared with the cost of the advertising.

There are bound to be some subjective and arbitrary assumptions involved in this kind of calculation, but we were not the first to have to put a price tag on this sort of thing. Health economists do it all the time, as the basis for investments in treatments, hospitals and staffing levels, and bodies such as NICE, the National Institute for Health and Clinical Excellence, face these questions every day of the year. NICE has a published guideline figure for the notional value of a QALY, a 'quality-adjusted life year' at full fitness, of £30,000.

The stroke campaign was striking and memorable, and the number of people going to hospital immediately did increase. If you looked at the overall cost savings and benefits to society over several years, it was clear that the payback was impressive, so it was not surprising that it was duly honoured with a gold award from the IPA.

I've been a judge for these IPA awards – as the analytics and econometrics specialist on the panel – and each time I've done it I've always felt that they are particularly worth while. The awards are based on detailed case study papers submitted by advertisers and their agencies that show how a problem has been tackled, what the solution was and what the demonstrable results and payoffs have been. All the papers, over a period of 30 years or more, are publicly available on a big IPA database – a fund of useful information for anyone who wants to know what advertising has really been able to achieve since the early 1980s. Campaigns like the best of the Department of Health initiatives can motivate change for the better and can produce objectively worthwhile payoffs, but nobody should take it on trust. The interesting point was that, until we started slicing and dicing the data and delving into these issues of value for money, very few people were critically assessing whether the department's campaign spend was delivering improved health outcomes and therefore paying back.

Justifying the investment in programmes like the Department of Health's is often difficult to do in the short term. But that may not be a fair yardstick. If awareness of a disease or its symptoms or what to do in an emergency can be raised once, that knowledge is likely to stick with people for a long time – certainly years, and possibly decades. We don't have a convincing way of capturing those very long-term benefits from public and health education and awareness campaigns, but they must exist at some level and they would obviously tend to add to the justification for the costs involved. To take a familiar British example, lives are probably being saved even now by RoSPA's old 'Clunk click every trip' seatbelts campaign that ran, in various forms, from 1971 right through to 1998.

The Department of Health was being quite forward thinking in taking the trouble to analyse the impact of its publicity work. Most public sector bodies don't bother. But because the DH is a huge spender, taking the lion's share of the money the government spends on marketing, it needs to provide evidence to back up its budget requirements. Before the recession, the government had the UK's biggest marketing spend, totalling more than £250 million. When spending cuts hit home, in 2010, and the government's advertising budget was cut by half, it was still the fifth largest advertiser, spending as much as the Asda supermarket chain.

What we were trying to do for the Department of Health was to find out whether the money spent on marketing communications could change attitudes and lead to a positive long-term behaviour change.

It was interesting trying to bring the disciplines I was used to deploying outside into the unfamiliar, politicised ethos of Whitehall, and I learned a lot from my work with the civil service. It made me revise a lot of unconscious stereotypes I had accumulated. I suppose I'd assumed all Whitehall civil servants would be out of the same bag. But they're not at all. It quickly struck me that the civil service was a very broad church, with a surprising range of characters, backgrounds and assumptions. Many people, I could see, had their own opinions and didn't necessarily agree with what was being done or how money was being spent. In the end, they would have to do what they were told, but there was more of a fight going on behind some of the spending and prioritisation decisions than I would ever have realised.

Of course, there were also some elements that would be familiar to anyone who has ever watched an episode of *Yes, Minister*. As one senior man told me: 'You get some minister or other rushing in with some harebrained, crazy scheme he's dreamed up to get a headline or two and it's up to us to try to put him off before any damage is done.'

But these efforts seemed, as far as I could tell, to be mostly benign, rather than Machiavellian. The people involved were, on the whole, quite impressive, conscientious and simply trying to do a good job. It seemed obvious that it was usually the politicians who would shoot from the hip, set all sorts of hares running and then not be around to deal with the consequences.

Though Whitehall was a great experience, I noticed that I felt some sense of relief each time I stepped back into my usual business world. We may not have achieved the heights of rational marketing yet, but at least, in the private sector, the logic of the marketplace gives you some basic certainties you can cling on to.

*'Decentralisation actually leads to more information
being taken into account'
— Friedrich Hayek*

CHAPTER 12

What Do You Do When the Data's Not There?

How my version of the Delphi process can squeeze good forecasts out of group consultations in situations where the usual business data simply isn't available. Nobody said it was going to be easy.

Because most of my early globetrotting had been done on behalf of SmithKline Beecham, I became deeply involved in sales force optimisation issues, around the world, at the time of SKB's merger with Glaxo Wellcome, in 2000. Field sales forces are the key marketing tool in pharma and the industry spends heavily on putting them out there to meet doctors and nurses in what is seen as a semi-educational role.

Both SKB and Glaxo Wellcome were huge companies, each actively promoting maybe 12 products at a time. The sales force at each company would be divided into Team A, Team B and so on, and Team A would be responsible for promoting, say, products 1, 2 and 3 to hospitals and the secondary care channel (primary care would be GPs). A particular drug, an antibiotic, for example, might be a hospital product in its intravenous form but a primary care product as a capsule.

The newly-merged company needed to understand how

these sales teams were spending their time. In order to help optimise resources, we needed to know how they were allocating their efforts, how many calls they were making per day, who they were getting to see, how much time they would have with each person and how they would spend the time within each meeting. A sales rep might get in to see the doctor and spend five minutes of a 10-minute meeting talking about drug A and four minutes on drug B, with just a quick reminder, at the end, about drug C, along with handing over some samples or literature.

The new GlaxoSmithKline needed to get an accurate picture of all this to see where resources were really being spent. And resources – in the sales force context – means time, which has a cost to it, of course. We were trying to figure out realistically what the actual amount of resource allocated to each particular drug was over a given time period – usually the last year, maybe two years.

Both merging companies had had similar field sales set-ups, though they had developed very distinct cultures. Glaxo was decentralised, with a great deal of freedom for local managers to do what they judged best. Local Glaxo management could decide that drugs A, B and C were relevant for this market, while drugs D, E and F weren't and should get little or no time.

SmithKline Beecham was completely different – highly centralised, with global planning edicts which might just state from on high 'We want to sell drugs, A, C and F and de-emphasise the others.'

So you had different, competing models. There were two product portfolios, two sets of management teams and two sales forces, and we were trying to merge them together efficiently. Altogether, there was a total range of 20 or 30 products now, and the merged company needed to decide which ones it was going to emphasise and where it was going to place its bets.

The rational marketing approach to this kind of situation is to go through a process that says 'OK, if we placed our bets on Product A, what would the payback be?' This means employing some form of analytical modelling, where you look at past investment of resources and the payback from them, and using that to create a forecast. So the question is then, 'How do we build a good forecasting model? How do we know, when we're placing our bets for the next three years, what we'll get back?'

In the case of the Big Pharma merger, we decided to use any available data and analytics we could, in the normal way. But there were a lot of markets around the world where there was no reliable data, or even no data at all. We needed data down to the individual or local level, often called cross-sectional data. We needed the kind of specific data that would tell us 'This sales rep did 100 calls and these were the sales, but this rep did 50 calls and got this level of sales.'

In the territories where that kind of split was not available, we would usually find the only data was aggregated totals – 'I've got 100 sales reps in this country and this was my figure for total sales.' And that didn't help us much.

Nevertheless, even where we didn't have cross-sectional data we could use in the normal way, major investment decisions still needed to be made. We still needed to find a way of constructing a usable model to help us decide the optimal number of sales reps and how they should be deployed across consumer groups and product lines.

My own company at that time, Edge, had won the contract to carry out this analysis in markets all around the world, in every country outside the USA and Europe. That meant we were doing lots of work in the Far East and South America and in developing countries where there wasn't ever a chance of getting hold of detailed cross-sectional data.

Over the course of this long international project, because of the lack of data, we adapted and refined the use of a 'collective intelligence' wisdom-of-crowds-type technique, where we got people to estimate, as a group, what they thought the relationship would be between sales force activity and sales.

We would work with them to try to draw up a curve, where you could say 'If I put three reps on this, or six reps on this, or 10 reps on this, I should get sales that go up like this.'

This forecasting approach is known as the Delphi technique, or ETE (estimate-talk-estimate). It was originally developed in the 1950s by the RAND Corporation, an American think tank, and it has actually been designed and developed to avoid the kind of bias you might expect in this sort of exercise. In particular, it is designed to sidestep the obvious potential problems of group estimates, such as bandwagon jumping and halo effects.

The goal of a Delphi group is obviously to end up getting a forecast from the group as a whole. But the way you get there is to ask everyone involved to give individual opinions, feeding them into the process anonymously.

There are three essential components that are needed for a successful Delphi process. It must be informed, anonymous and iterative.

To make it informed, you bring in people who know about the products or the market and you make sure you give those taking part as much firm information as you possibly can about the history of the products and their past performance. But you don't only want experts and specialists, as their viewpoint may be too narrow and predetermined and influenced by groupthink. There is a value here in diversity and different perspectives. You'll usually end up with a mix that includes some people who have worked with the particular products before and others who haven't.

The process needs to be anonymous, as that is the only way to ensure that people say exactly what they believe to be true. If these informed people have doubts or negative concerns, it's very important that these are part of the recipe and are not suppressed for political reasons or for fear of the boss raising an eyebrow. We want to avoid the conformity that often appears in group situations.

But the real key to the success of the Delphi process is its iterative nature. You get people to have a go, to fill out what they think to start with. Then you bring the whole group together and display the results, so that everyone gets to see the whole spread of opinion.

You show the maximum answer, the minimum answer and the middle, the median answer, which, of course, gives each individual the opportunity to recognise where he or she is on this spectrum.

You may also hold a quick ballot, in the meeting, for participants to vote on who they think genuinely are experts in this area – though they may not be people whose status or job titles officially recognise their expertise – and then show everybody three experts' answers as well. These may or may not reflect the thrust of opinion shown in the main results display. And, of course, you often find that the nominated experts disagree with each other.

The basic idea is to capture a wide spread of different opinions to start with.

We used to do it by giving every person a computer with a graphing software package on it and getting them to estimate, as well as they could, how sales would rise and at what point the rise might start to flatten off, under a range of different scenarios. So each participant came up with a personal set of forecast estimates and a personal prediction for the shape of the curve. We would then put all these answers together and look at the group's estimates and forecasts as a whole.

The next step in the Delphi process is for the facilitator to begin to challenge and sound out each of the points of view.

I would start, perhaps, with the maximum forecast.

'What does this imply?' I'd ask. 'For sales to come out this high, what would have to happen?

'This (anonymous) person is saying that if we had 10 reps selling this product, we would get sales of £10 million. But we're only selling £5 million now, so how would we be able to double that? How's that going to work?'

So we'd start to tease it all apart and test the thinking and look at the implications of these guesses. I would challenge the forecasts that were being made, from a rational point of view. Quite often, too, people would pipe up in the discussion and reveal themselves.

'Actually, that was my number,' they'd say, 'and I think this is right, because…' And they'd give the argument for their point of view. Then other people would argue against their numbers, and, ideally, a lot of different views and reasons would get an airing in the meeting. That was always an initial goal for the facilitator, to flush out different views and reasons at this stage, and get the people in the group to start testing them against each other.

Once this had gone on for a while, I would call a halt and give everyone a second chance to rebutton the cloak of anonymity and draw the curve representing likely sales with three reps, six reps and 10 reps all over again.

Some people would draw exactly what they had drawn before. Others would have been persuaded by the arguments they'd heard, or would simply decide that they had been too optimistic or pessimistic in the first round. When the results were in, the one near-certainty was always that they wouldn't look the same as those from the previous iteration. Often, you'd see a certain amount of convergence. The maximum and minimum might have moved in towards the middle, leaving the spread less wide than it was before, as the extreme optimists and extreme pessimists both thought again and modified their opinions.

At the very end of the process, we would finally take the median answer – the middle answer within the group – as representing the best estimate the group, as a whole, was able to come up with.

This wouldn't be what lay people generally think of as the average, the arithmetic mean that you'd get by adding up all the estimated sales numbers and dividing by the number of people in the group. That would be influenced and skewed by the extremes, up or down. The median isn't. If you just take the middle number, it doesn't matter if some hothead has got carried away and put in 180, when everyone else put in figures between 30 and 100.

That's not to say that the people at the extremes may not be right, or at least have a serious point of view. If someone is right out on a limb like that, we want them to stand up and make their point and argue their case. Perhaps they are right and everyone else is wrong. Sometimes the impassioned extremists are able to win others over and move them towards their point of view. And, of course, if they move enough people towards them, that will shift the median value – the value we're ultimately taking as the group's best guess – in their direction.

What sometimes took people by surprise about this process was how seriously we meant it when we said it was iterative. We'd go round again and again, sometimes going through four or five rounds of the discussion process. We'd lock 15, 20, sometimes even 30 people away in a hotel for three days at a time, for a string of gruelling sessions that would often leave them completely drained and wrung out.

We'd get them going early in the morning and keep them at it till late at night. With maybe 20 different products to get through for the merged company, these marathons were as much a test of stamina as an intellectual exercise.

But sessions like this are actually brilliant planning tools. They bring out so much information about your products and markets – and also about your people. There's no stone unturned and no room to hide. You get to see, sometimes all too clearly, just how well prepared, or otherwise, the individuals are. I've known instances where people have been fired after these sessions, because, without their support staff to cover for them, they've been exposed as just not up to the job.

Normally though, after we'd done one of these projects, I'd go and sit down for a beer with the general manager and we'd have a chat about what had gone on. There'd often be a sense of achievement, of a job well done and a team that worked well together. But sometimes it would be different.

'What do you think of my sales director?' the general manager would ask. 'Well,' I'd say, 'he didn't perform very well, did he?'

'No, he didn't. I didn't know. I didn't realise he wasn't on top of everything like that.' And the weak link sales director would go, or at least be moved sideways to some other role where his incompetence could do less harm.

In the end, the primary output from this demanding process would be the median estimate I mentioned before, which would be taken as the basis for the forecasting model. We would try to crank through every product in the portfolio and build a realistic model for each product to enable us to optimise the allocation of the available resources.

Once we had used these group sessions to derive a response curve, just like the ones shown in Chapter 7, all of our usual optimisation techniques could be used to work out how to get the best returns from the sales force.

In the case of SmithKline Beecham and Glaxo, the merger was bringing together enormous numbers of people, most of them with very little knowledge of the other company's products and their strengths and weaknesses. We would be going through our Delphi process in a big room with a lot of people who might not know each other at all, so that, at one level, it could be seen as a teambuilding exercise.

There was definitely some value in this, as people got to know about the people from the other team very quickly, and about the products. But what was even more important was the process of deciding, for the new, combined team, where the bets were going to be placed. For the collective management team, these were the key decisions that needed to be taken. But nobody, by definition, had seen both halves of the equation. And the one thing the newly merged GlaxoSmithKline could not afford was to allow people to do their own thing in isolation from the larger, joint company.

The variation, from country to country and market to market, was enormous. In some markets, the merger of these two pharmaceutical giants worked well straight away and the people got on famously, right from the start. In other markets, they really struggled with the cultural differences and the personalities involved.

After all this effort, big decisions had to be made. The conclusions might have major and potentially disruptive ramifications within individual territories or even worldwide.

The experts, collectively, would be concluding that, say, products A, B and C from SmithKline Beecham and products X, Y and Z from Glaxo should be included in the merged company's future planning. Those decisions had implications for production units, for marketing budgets, for people's jobs, even for patient welfare in some cases. They weren't random decisions, but you could never be sure, till afterwards, that they were right.

Again, as always, it was a question of where the company should be placing its bets. If a slimmed-down product line-up that revolved round products A, B, C, X, Y and Z was forecast to give the best chance of maximising profits, that was the direction the business logic would oblige the company to follow.

It wasn't always quite as clear cut as that, though. Sometimes the conclusions of the collective forecasting process suited the local managers that had come from the Glaxo side, but were in head-on conflict with the global policies handed down from the centre by top management at SmithKline Beecham. When the cultures clashed, there were tensions, and sometimes casualties. The ultimate decision would then depend on how successfully the local managers could sell their ideas up the management chain towards the centres of power. Sometimes they could, and everyone would move forward in the direction that had emerged from our deliberations. At other times, local managers were told their views and forecasts had been noted but were not being adopted.

Large companies are almost invariably organised along standardised lines. One person will be responsible for a particular marketing channel – the sales force, perhaps, or television – or for a particular product line. If you think of a matrix that brings together products on one axis and marketing activity on the other, every cell of that matrix is going to be owned by somebody, by an individual.

So when you come out with the conclusions from a forecasting process and say 'The best bet will be to take part of the television spend on product A and move it across to spend that money on radio advertising for product C', you can be pretty sure that this recommendation will not be universally popular.

There will be winners, quietly delighted that their products will benefit and that their job security is assured for the next year or two. They won't be saying very much. And there will be losers, who stand to suffer from the changes that are likely to follow. You're taking money from Fred and giving it to Bill, and, suddenly, Fred, even if he was enthusiastically involved in the earlier stages of the Delphi process, is twisting and turning and trying to find some reason why it should not be so.

How strong and ingenious the defence of this position is will depend on the intelligence and resourcefulness of the Fred in question. I've seen straightforward sulks and tantrums, pleading and aggression, flailing attacks on me, the process, the maths, the gods, everything. And I've seen the cooler, more calculating operators, who know, however much they are seething inside, that any apparent display of emotion will be seen as a sign of the weakness of their case. These Freds will be looking for good, rational arguments to support the status quo. And they generally recognise that that is best done by pulling into the debate some powerful external factor that simply was not there to be considered in the original process.

So they will accept the value and integrity of all we've been through to reach our predictions, but point out, regretfully, that the company is irrevocably and expensively committed to certain arrangements that would make it fearfully costly and damaging to follow the logic of the forecasts. Other, lesser people in the Delphi group may not have been privy to the business agreements or political understandings that need to be taken into account. There may be wheels within wheels. Contracted suppliers or joint venture partners may have an effective veto, or there may be key stakeholders – governments, perhaps – that would not appreciate this kind of change.

Less sophisticated Freds will sometimes mount a full frontal attack on the process and the numbers, pointing out that they consistently disagreed with 'those idiots in the room', who refused to be swayed by arguments they just didn't know enough to understand.

'I always had a different set of answers,' they'll say, 'and mine were informed estimates, not wild, optimistic guesses based on untested assumptions.'

As the facilitator, you will have observed whether these Freds really fought vehemently against the tide of opinion at the time, and you'll probably have a good idea whether this strong reaction now has actually been triggered by the belated realisation that their interests – and maybe even their jobs – are under threat.

One technique for dealing with this kind of assault is to use the recorded data from the sessions. In cases like this, I would go back to my room, check through the answers put forward by this particular individual in the course of the Delphi process, do a quick recalculation, and see what would happen to the conclusions if this Fred's own numbers were used, instead of the median figures derived from the whole group.

Very often, the result would not be materially different and I would know that Fred's position could be shown to be indefensible. I've always felt that I should handle these conflicts as gently, privately and gracefully as possible, so I would quietly take the guy to one side and tell him, before he made any further song and dance about it, that even substituting his own answers would not change the conclusions. There's no pleasure in ending the argument with a killer blow like that, but at least holding this kind of trump card usually guaranteed that this man's disappointment would not be brought up again and again and made the subject of a public battle.

Of course, given an adequate amount of time-series data, I would always opt for the fact-based objectivity of modelling, rather than the more subjective – and often highly stressful – process of running Delphi groups.

In the hands of a skilled operator, the Delphi methodology is surprisingly effective at creating something out of nothing. But the cost of having a large group of people, usually including a lot of fairly senior managers, corralled in a series of workshops for days on end and unable to do their normal work is far from negligible. It could easily amount to more than the cost of equipping the marketing department with its own desktop modelling software. That is not the point, though. Where suitable data is available, modelling is always the better option, and the one that is more likely to deliver profitable, quantified insights.

It is also, paradoxically, less likely to create so many tensions and antagonisms within a team. The truths that emerge may be just as uncomfortable, at times, but most people will know instinctively that they can't fight the cold, hard facts.

'The best way to predict the future is to invent it'
– Alan Kay

CHAPTER 13

On the Edge of the Future

Put the right modelling tools in the hands of the right people and you have the basis for a data-driven business revolution. Goodbye raindancing, hello rational marketing.

If there was one thing that became clear to me over the first twenty years of my career – with organisations like ZS Associates, the Henley Centre, Edge and Accenture – it was that the demand for marketing mix modelling was a growing trend, but that there were simply not enough rocket scientists to do the work.

As marketingQED developed, we began to realise that we had taken on something more significant than just refining the techniques and practice of modelling. As our focus became sharper, we began to understand that we had embarked on an important mission – to bring rational marketing to the widest possible business audience.

We knew that analysis could deliver great value to clients if they took on board what the analysts told them. Unfortunately, they often didn't, because it wasn't communicated to them in a way they understood.

We realised that it often took months to deliver results and that this meant that only slow-moving questions could be addressed. Everyday questions and decisions were left in the realms of gut feel and raindancing.

And, above all, we knew that modelling was expensive. You needed lots of fancy people for long periods of time. We could see that a better solution was needed.

The new idea was for an analytical software package that didn't exist. It occurred to us that the way forward could involve producing and selling a product that would put all that capacity and power into non-specialists' hands.

We thought it should be possible to write modelling software that would capture everything we knew about analytics and use advanced techniques to produce answers to the key questions in marketing.

What if we could use real historical information about sales, campaigns, pricing, seasonal factors, competitor activity and so on to make good, quick analyses of past marketing performance and accurate forecasts of future marketing effectiveness?

We would take a super modeller's years of experience and bottle it all up so that it could be used by anyone. We would give marketers their very own genie in a lamp.

We needed to produce usable, intuitive tools that would do the things the rocket scientists would do, but that could be driven by non-specialists. We wanted tools that could be used by ordinary marketing people who needed quick and illuminating answers to their questions about the options that were open to them.

The tools we envisaged would fall into two categories. The first consisted of tools to analyse and model what had happened in the past. The second – the more obviously sexy category – was about developing tools that would use these models to predict future performance and help people make the right business choices. That would involve forward-looking functions like forecasting and optimising marketing decisions.

That's the revolution in a nutshell.

We used to be the priesthood, the holders of knowledge, the statistical aristocracy who could call the shots and name our price.

Now we are democratising the access to this knowledge, flinging open the doors of the temple and letting the people in.

The product we've developed today is a straightforward shrink-wrapped software suite that offers out-of-the-box performance for non-experts. It's not even expensive in absolute terms, let alone in terms of the phenomenal payback companies can gain from improving their marketing effectiveness and their day-to-day tactical decisions. It unlocks a new era of rational marketing that can generate millions in sales and profit.

And we have done it. People who see it cannot quite believe that we have made modelling accessible. But we have.

Of course, it hasn't been easy. It's been a huge challenge to design a tool that's not much harder to handle than the elements of Microsoft Office. A lot of software companies can come up with bright ideas and knock up rough and ready kit. It's a great deal more difficult than it looks to move on from that and produce something that's stable, predictable, polished and genuinely easy to use.

As the CEO, I am concerned now with building up marketingQED. I'm busy trying to introduce the world to the startling idea that you really can put together an integrated marketing mix modelling toolkit that offers considerable power, sophistication and finesse, but that can easily be picked up and used by marketers, rather than mathematicians.

I am also making a broader plea for recognition of the idea of 'rational marketing' and an end to the raindancing culture that continues to waste so much marketing effort and money.

We all have access now to huge amounts of data. The sales of our products send us millions of messages from the market that we can track and collate – about what people want, when and how they want to buy it, and how they're responding to price changes and advertising campaigns.

We have the tools to help us tell when there's a real causal connection between our marketing activity and our sales performance, and to warn us when coincidences and misleading correlations threaten to send us off in the wrong direction. We can model and isolate the factors that have affected our performance in the past and use this knowledge to make accurate predictions to inform future decisions and optimise future spending.

We have everything we need to make rational marketing work for us.

My mission for the years to come is to persuade the world that this is a revolution that really does have to happen. It's needed, it's wanted, and it's available – for every industry and every company, from the grandest multinationals to the smallest local businesses.

Further Reading

- *Advertising Works 17*, Institute of Practitioners in Advertising – edited by Neil Dawson (World Advertising Research Center, 2009)
- *Advertising Works 19*, Institute of Practitioners in Advertising – edited by David Golding (Warc, 2010)
- *Competing on Analytics: The New Science of Winning,* Thomas H Davenport and Jeanne G Harris (Harvard Business School Press, 2007)
- *Improving Marketing Effectiveness,* Chartered Institute of Marketing and Deloitte (Chartered Institute of Marketing, 2010)
- *Marketing Accountability: A New Metrics Model to Measure Marketing Effectiveness,* Malcolm McDonald and Peter Mouncey (Kogan Page, 2011)
- *Marketing Payback: Is Your Marketing Profitable?*, Robert Shaw and David Merrick (Financial Times/Prentice Hall, 2005)
- *Moneyball,* Michael Lewis (W W Norton, 2004)
- *Super Crunchers: How Anything Can Be Predicted,* Ian Ayres (John Murray, 2007)
- *The Wisdom of Crowds,* James Surowiecki (Little, Brown, 2004)
- *Why Societies Need Dissent,* Cass R Sunstein (Harvard University Press, 2003)

Acknowledgements

So many people and companies – some named, others tactfully anonymised – have contributed, wittingly or unwittingly, to the ideas developed in *Raindancing*. I'd like to thank them all, but particular thanks must go to my wife, Tracey, to my colleagues John Dawson, Drew Barnes, Katy Taylor, Diane Easterbrook, Phil Williams and Jessica Bahia, to Joyce Kelso at the IPA, to Chloé Scaplehorn and Graham Tilley, to Clare 'The Book Guru' Christian and to Ian Shircore, for his help and advice in making this book happen.

Index